A Love Letter To The Nations

# Magnanimous Love

The Key to Transforming a City!

Edited by Patricia Dextrom, Dennis Moore, Anne Cody
and Jacqueline Dominguez

# TABLE OF CONTENTS

# APPENDIX

A Journey to Loving Magnanimously
Companion Study Guide

# ENDORSEMENTS

"Stephanie is a true leader. Her life and her life's work have pointed in one direction: unity. I will personally follow her leadership and consider her a valuable resource."

Christopher Brooks
VP of Human Resources & Development at Shine/Merge Twin Cities

"Stephanie leads one of the most well-run, organized and effective city movements I've seen in the country."

Jim Morgan
President and Founder of Meet The Need Ministries

"Stephanie remembers who she is, her roots, and the changes and miracles she has seen."

Matthew Philip
Director of Global Outreach at Trinity Church

"Stephanie is an insightful and talented leader who is master at collaborative teamwork"

Dennis Moore
Ministry Coach with MCMD

"Stephanie is an apostolic voice for such a time as this. She radiates oneness with the Father, is in love with the Son, and is in constant fellowship with the Holy Spirit."

Natalie Willmarth,<br>
Board Member of Catalyst Ministries

"Magnanimous...now that's a fun word to say. Say it three times fast and it's even more fun. However, beyond the linguistic tongue tying fun, is the deep challenge of unpacking its meaning when connected with love in the context of city transformation and church unity. Stephanie Butler does a marvelous job of showing how magnanimous love lived out through COGL Network transformed her life as a leader and the church and city she loves. This is a wonderful book for those with a heart for their city and a desire to see denominations work together for its transformation."

Darrell Maclearn,<br>
Founder of the Nazarene Organic Church Network

"There are very few who share such passion, give so generously, love so unconditionally, believe so strongly, live so freely, and speak so powerfully. She is uniquely created as a humble catalyst of change and transforming voice to God's people...listen, learn, and your life will never be the same."

Jeffery Brown,<br>
CEO of Inspire Care &<br>
Chairman of Uplift Our Youth Foundation

# DEDICATION

This book is dedicated to my natural and spiritual families. My mother whose courage, perseverance, and grit taught and prepared me well for all that God had planned for me. My step-father who taught me what the heart of Father God and a true spirit of adoption looks like. My husband and best friend whose patience, authentic love, generosity and humor kept me hopeful and laughing as I died daily that Christ may live. Our children whose purity, hunger, zeal and courage inspire me regularly.

And to Janice & Vince Parris and the many precious leaders and friends who served on our board, both board members and board member emeritus, who loved me through my prideful idealistic seasons and gave generously, graciously and gloriously to see something beyond our own dreams built. What a joy to partner with God to build something that gives glory to His name alone! To Trinity Church staff and elders for taking a chance on a wildly idealistic young woman. You all have invested so much in me and our community. I am eternally grateful.

To Patty, Dennis, Anne and Jacqueline who edited the manuscript time and again. You are amazing! The Kingdom leaders who are a part of each team, so faithfully giving of your time, treasure and talent. You are the premier example of living magnanimously. God is changing the culture of our city because each of you. You have faithfully responded to His voice as you have simply said what He's told you to say and done what He's shown you to do.

Thank you, Good Cities Glenn, Eric and Reggie, for your constant encouragement. To Angela Austin, Adam Williams, Sean Holland and Melvin Jones for your friendship, perseverance and courage to continue running together and choosing to love again and again.

Finally, to my precious prayer partners and church family at Shekhinah International, especially Laura and also Wendy and Carole. God has taught us so much about how to love each other and others. The truth is without the gift of each of you, I never would have fulfilled this aspect God's plan for me. I thank God for you often! I pray this book encourages those mentioned here as so often God has used each of you to encourage me to continue on in His very best. Now on the flip side I can say He was worth it, and He is worth so much more.

# NOTE FROM THE AUTHOR

Beloved,

In February 2018, I attended the Turn Around Conference in Washington, DC, where a leader shared that we needed another love letter from the Irish to stir us up again. They were pointing to the Welsh revival as the birthplace of all the revivals we have experienced in America and the cities across the world. Upon hearing those words, I couldn't contain my tears, knowing I had just finished this book and that I have an Irish-American heritage. In that moment, Holy Spirit nudged my spirit with a sense that this book, Magnanimous Love, is just that— a love letter to the church in this nation and the nations around the world. It is a picture of Father's call bidding His children to press in; to love well; to live sacrificially; to build His kingdom; and to serve our brothers, sisters and cities in a way that proclaims both the gospel of salvation and the gospel of the kingdom. Now is the time.

I pray God baptizes His church in America and abroad afresh with Holy Spirit, fire, glory and grace so that we can sincerely proclaim "as Christ is so are we in this world" (John 4:17). It is our greatest privilege to be gloriously wrecked and rebuilt by the Master of Magnanimous Love - our Father God. I pray you are deeply blessed as you read through the pages herein.

In His Ever-abounding Grace,
Stephanie Butler

# Chapter 1
## ONE WORD

It was a morning like any other. As I lay in bed, my mind was still a bit foggy when my iPhone began to play the mellow chimes ringtone to wake me from a much-needed, six-hour recharge. The chimes started off soothing and soft. They were honestly enjoyable at first until the fog began to lift and I could hear more clearly that they were increasing in volume with each new round. It was obvious my flesh was waking up because I immediately began to think, *Ughhhh, Lord, do I have to get up?* God is so gracious. I was impressed with the thought, *Do you want to get up?* I thought, *yes (long exhale), yes I do.* I then proceeded with my mundane morning routine, which ensured there wouldn't be any unnecessary interruptions in the middle of my quiet time with the Lord. If there is one thing of which I have become painfully aware, it is that without my Jesus time in the morning, I tend not to be a very good ambassador for Him throughout the day.

That particular morning, I was feeling a bit stagnant. If I'm being completely honest, I was in a bit of a funk. It wasn't quite a midlife crisis, but an Abraham moment where I needed to absolutely surrender my ministry dreams back to Father God, yet again. I had a BHAG (Big HAIRY Audacious Goal): I wanted leaders in our city to be united in five years' time. BHAG, according to Jim Collins and Jerry Porras, the authors of *Good to Great*, is a strategic business statement, similar to a vision statement, that is created to focus an organization on a single, medium-to-long-term, organization-wide goal that is audacious

1

and likely to be externally questionable but not internally regarded as impossible.

I dared to believe we could equip and encourage God's army to resolutely rise up across denominational lines to push back the enemy and advance God's kingdom with considerable, united resolve. The reality was, we had taken some ground, but I was naive in my estimation of the time it would require to begin to make real progress. With such a huge goal, I was feeling slightly stuck, stifled and restless.

The lion's share of the leaders involved had more questions, concerns and personal agendas than resolve. *How do you plan to transform an entire city? What does this mean for me personally and for my ministry? How can I be a part of what you are doing and still be obedient to my personal call?* A few people I trusted even asked others, Who *does she think she is? What qualifies her to lead this?* It was a crucial crossroad where many of the leaders were struggling with their significance and vying for influence and control in the midst of a transitional year.

Even though their questions pricked against my passionate pursuits, I knew they were valid and even relevant. I was certain I needed to be able to clearly communicate the heart of God as I answered each one, but I was at a loss as to how to do it because everything seemed so clear to me. I was struggling with understanding how others couldn't see it as clearly as I did. I was in leadership crisis. In addition to the questions from others, I myself was looking at my experience and beginning to question my own qualifications. My particular ministry journey hadn't exactly followed the standard leadership track of so many of my ministry peers.

I hadn't gone to seminary as most traditional church leaders did. In fact, while at Trinity Church, an opportunity for theological training was very graciously offered to me and I was excited about the potential to move in that direction. However, when I prayed about it the answer I received, much to my dismay, was *absolutely not!* I was caught off guard, I thought for sure that was the fast track to ministry success and I would surely be able to change the world once I checked that off my list. Traditional seminary and theological training are extremely helpful and excellent preparation for ministry. Nonetheless, Father God simply did not want me to take that particular path of development. Instead, Biblical training has come through my personal Bible study time and working with leaders and Christian friends He has placed in my life over the years.

In addition to teaching me spiritual principles through mentors and friends year after year, God would open ministry doors and give me the opportunity to develop my spiritual gifts of leadership and discernment by helping ministries define their purpose and raise up new leaders. Between 2002 and 2012 I had the privilege of helping eight different ministries clarify their vision and establish leadership teams to carry on the work of moving the ministry forward.

During those valuable years of being prepared by God, I had learned it was imperative to move beyond a posture of questioning God's methods fairly quickly or I could inadvertently spiral into a season of discouragement. That being said, whenever my day starts with a seemingly unanswerable question, I have learned that is a good time to reflect on the many words God has whispered to my heart in the past.

# A GENTLE WHISPER

Whispers are a funny thing. They are quiet and intimate and, if we are not careful to capture them, they can be quickly forgotten amidst the clamoring voices striving for our attention on a daily basis. In 1 Kings 19:1-14, Elijah is an example of someone who almost missed the whisper God had for him. He just wanted to escape and with good reason — there was a bounty on his head. But rather than console him, the voice of the Lord asked him, "What are you doing here, Elijah?" Then the Lord continued and said, "Go out and stand in the presence of the Lord." In other words, the solution to his problem wasn't necessarily changing geographical locations, but perhaps coming out of hiding. It would be found in a single encounter with the Lord, in a single word gently whispered from God's heart to his. In the Scripture above, the whisper followed the fire. Those of us who have endured the fiery furnace of affliction often deeply treasure these whispers because we are intimately acquainted with the cost of having obtained them. A whisper from the heart of God is one of the treasures we are called to seek out as his daughters and sons! Proverbs 25:2 states, "It is the glory of God to conceal a matter; to search out a matter is the glory of kings." God so often speaks in whispers because the journey of discovery is the very thing that reveals His greatness to us and through us.

As I started my prayer time that morning, I picked up my journal and thumbed through the pages, reviewing many of the words God had gently whispered to my heart over the years. While I was encouraged by God's very words, promises and victories recorded, nothing was completely settling the uneasiness I was feeling until I carefully considered the timeline in the very back of my journal. The truth is, I was convicted as much as I was comforted. I immediately noticed how God had so faithfully guided me into greater measures of joy, peace, wholeness and adventure year after year. It became crystal clear that He had always transitioned me in perfect timing from one season of service into the next. The reality began to register: It was 2014, and I had only been serving with my current ministry for six short years. As I reminisced about my walk, I recalled how long it took for me to allow God to work His love into my heart. I started to feel that peace, the one that makes no sense in light of the circumstances you see all around you. The one mentioned in Philippians 4:4-7, "Rejoice in the Lord always, I will say again rejoice! Let your gentleness be evident to all. The Lord is near. Do not be anxious about anything but in every situation, by prayer and petition, with thanksgiving, present your requests to God. And the peace of God, which transcends all understanding, will guard your hearts and minds in Christ Jesus!" Conviction, courage and faith began to rise up in my heart and I thought, *perhaps we are right on track.* When I considered it from His perspective, six years was not even a blip on the screen of eternity; it wasn't even a decade. In fact, if it were to be compared to the lifespan of a human child, the child would only be in his or her first grade class or perhaps even kindergarten. With that context in mind, my heart began to settle a bit, so I took a deep breath and asked God, *So then, what's next?* My questioning had shifted from asking if I was supposed to be the one doing this to asking God, *How do we get unstuck?* And *How*

5

*do I love your precious children sincerely while some are intentionally and unintentionally wounding me by questioning my abilities and calling?*

Most days the questions and remarks of my fellow laborers didn't bother me, but that morning, I felt at a loss as to how to love them the way Jesus would. It became very apparent that we were all still in process. They were simply trying to understand their roles and find a place in this huge dream to transform our city, and I was trying not to mess it up! They needed a better understanding of where we were going. I needed a bit more courage to continue advancing God's kingdom and loving some who seemed to have it out for me.

# Chapter 2
## MAGNANIMOUS

So I asked God a simple question, *Father, is there anything you want to say to me today?* There was a brief pause and I closed my eyes, attempting to be as still as possible so I could hear even the faintest whisper within. A few moments later the word *magnanimous* came up. I thought it was strange because my understanding of magnanimous at the time was that it simply meant generous. Thrilled at the possibility of having received my answer, I quickly looked up the definition on my phone. Much to my surprise, the following definitions appeared:

Dictionary.com

1. To be generous in forgiving an insult or injury, free from petty resentfulness or vindictiveness, *especially toward those who have malicious intent toward you* (emphasis mine). Example: To be magnanimous toward one's enemies.
2. To be high-minded or noble. Example: He/she is a just and magnanimous ruler.
3. Proceeding from or revealing generosity or nobility of mind or character.

Google.com

1. To be very generous or forgiving, especially toward a rival or someone less powerful than oneself.

2.  Synonyms: generous, charitable, benevolent, beneficent, big-hearted, handsome, princely, altruistic, philanthropic, unselfish, chivalrous, noble, forgiving, merciful, lenient, indulgent, or clement.

I was astonished! There was my answer. I had asked God how to love his children when some of them were intentionally trying to harm me and His answer was to love them *magnanimously!* Love them generously, unselfishly, leniently without resentment, forgiving insults, forgiving those who are intentionally trying to bring me harm. I suddenly felt like the Apostle Peter when he asked Jesus, "Lord how many times must I forgive my brother or sister who sins against me, up to seven times?" (Matthew 18:21-22). And the Lord graciously responded, "I tell you not seven times, but seventy-seven times." I had read that verse countless times. I had studied the love of God for several years. I had memorized Matthew 5:44, "Love your enemies and pray for those who persecute you." But something new stood out as I re-examined the verse in context that day. Matthew 5:43-48 says, "You have heard that it was said, 'Love your neighbor and hate your enemy. But I tell you, love your enemies and pray for those who persecute you, that you may be children of your Father in heaven. He causes His sun to rise on the evil and the good, and sends rain on the righteous and the unrighteous. If you love those who love you, what reward will you get? Are not even the tax collectors doing that? And if you greet only your own people, what are you doing more than others? Do not even pagans do that? Be perfect, therefore, as your heavenly Father is perfect.'" It was as if He were saying, *I don't want you to just love them. I want you to practice magnanimous love. I want you to love them perfectly. Love them like I love you.* In that moment, I was reminded of the new commandment Jesus gave us, one I had recited many times, but this morning it resonated in my soul with new substance, significance and sobriety. John 13:34, "A new command I give you: Love one another. As I have loved you, *so you must* love one another" (emphasis mine). I had certainly been praying for these leaders, and I was most definitely being kind. I had forgiven them as well and would continue to do that, but I wasn't intentionally blessing them. I couldn't say I was being generous toward those who were causing the problems. Truth be told, I would at times withdraw a bit in an effort to not be hurt, but Father God was asking me to press in and pour out such a blessing that they couldn't contain it. He was challenging me to come up higher, to love like He has loved me: extravagantly, benevolently and magnanimously. His challenge to me that morning was to love perfectly. As I continued researching the word *magnanimous* online, I found another definition that pierced my heart:

Vocabulary.com

1. Magnanimous comes from the Latin magnus meaning "great" and animus meaning "soul."

So literally magnanimous means *"great soul."* I was completely blown away. His literal answer to my question of how to love them was *"great soul love."* I had to laugh out loud. Having done extensive studies in preparation for sermons on the body, soul and spirit of man, I knew that the soul is comprised of our mind, will and emotions. It is literally our decision-making center. It is the place where spiritual battles are either won or lost. As I pondered those words, I understood what He was saying, *Stephanie, you need to get my perfect love for others to move from your mind into your will and emotions. Let it permeate your soul, which in turn will make it great!*

That morning I realized there was still a small part of me that longed for earthly justice, sort of like James and John, the sons of thunder. Do you remember their story? Luke 9:51-55, "As the time approached for Him to be taken up to heaven, Jesus resolutely set out for Jerusalem. And He sent messengers on ahead, who went into a Samaritan village to get things ready for him; but the people there did not welcome Him, because He was heading for Jerusalem. When the disciples James and John saw this, they asked, 'Lord, do you want us to call fire down from heaven to destroy them?' But Jesus turned and rebuked them. Then He and His disciples went to another village." James and John were quick to point out that the people weren't helping with the mission and to ask if the Lord wanted them to pray to take them out. It says that He rebuked them. This request actually had biblical precedence. The location they were in was the very location where the prophet Elijah had called down fire on the armies of king Ahaziah who rejected and threatened the messenger of the Lord. After calling fire down from heaven on King Ahaziah's two captains and their 50 troops, the third captain pleaded with Elijah "See, fire has fallen from heaven and consumed the first two captains and all their men. But now have respect for my life!" (2 Kings 1:10-14). The disciples thought they were following the biblical pattern of a powerful man of God!

Jesus had to sternly remind them why He was there — to seek and save the lost. These two disciples were so zealous to help Jesus they thought it would be a good idea to destroy the very people He came to save. Oy vey! Imagine the patience, the love, the endurance it took to equip these sons of thunder. They had so much potential and yet so much to learn. Imagine the intentional time it took to teach them how to love people.

The very thought of this comforted me in light of my own slowness to learn. As I continued to reflect upon the final days of both James and John and how they each courageously gave their lives for the sake of the elect, the glory of God, and the honor of Jesus, it gave me deep conviction and hope that I, too, could do the same. Acts 12:2 tells us that King Herod had "James, the brother of John, put to death with the sword." Revelation 1:9 tells us that the Apostle John was exiled for his faith, "I, John, your brother and companion in the suffering and kingdom and patient endurance that are ours in Jesus, was on the island of Patmos because of the word of God and the testimony of Jesus." My own experience and struggle, of course, can't compare to the persecution they suffered, but their courage emboldened my heart all the same.

## GREAT-HEARTED GENERAL

The final definition I found for magnanimous that early morning, shook me to the core. It read as follows:

Thefreedictionary.com

1. Noble and generous in spirit, a great-hearted general, a magnanimous conqueror.
2. Generous, understanding, and tolerant, "a heart big enough to hold no grudges."
3. Willing to give of one's self and one's possessions.

It was as if God were saying to me in that moment, *I am the great-hearted General! Do you truly want to be one of my generals? Then you, too, must be great-hearted! And if you want to be great-hearted, you must learn to walk in magnanimous love. You must hold no grudges and give yourself fully and give your own possessions as well.* I was taken aback by the terminology God was using and the fear of God fell upon me. It was thick, startling, and made me a bit uneasy, yet I was excited at the same time; however, I didn't dare say a word. I was unnerved that the definition of *magnanimous* included the term a *great-hearted general.* Several years earlier someone had shared a very similar word for me during a prayer meeting.

It was on March 3, 2002, that God first began to cultivate this idea of being a general in my heart. I had been learning that God created each one of us for a specific purpose and how each one of us had a personal call to a very specific work. Ephesians 2:10 states, "We are God's handiwork, created in Christ Jesus to do good works, which God has prepared in advance for us to do." That beautiful spring day I was yearning to know why He had created me. I was asking Him, *Father, what purpose did you make me for?* I was enamored with our Lord and all He had done for me. I had been brokenhearted, but He had healed me with His perfect love and forgiveness. I had been confused, but He had given me His good and precious promises leading me into a life of blessing and hope. I had felt alone and lost, but he had shown me I belonged to His family. I had been fatherless, but He had become my perfect Father! I wanted so desperately to discover what the good works were that the Apostle Paul was referring to in Ephesians; not just any works, but the very ones He had prepared in advance for me to do.

So, I prayed. A lot! Often for several hours a day. There had been this nagging void in me that I couldn't shake. It couldn't be satisfied by the idea of just serving Him. He is worthy of so much more. He is deserving of our everything. I couldn't bear the idea of a trite, nonchalant, careless offering of service in light of everything He had done for me on the cross. I had asked this question in various ways before: *Who am I? What is my part? Why did you create me? What am I supposed to be doing right now?* Up to this point, I had only gotten a word on unity from 1 Corinthians 12:12-28, which at that time was just starting to make sense. I knew my call had something to do with the challenge Paul was giving in Corinthians to the church to be one, to honor one another. But I was not clear as to my role in our generation. It seemed out of reach and somewhat unattainable and I initially had no idea what to do next.

But that particular day in March, I was re-reading Francis Frangipane's book *The Three Battle Grounds.* In chapter 12, called The *Repairers of the Breach,* Frangipane referenced Isaiah 58:12, which says, "And those from among you will rebuild the ancient ruins; you will raise up the age-old foundations; and you will be called the repairer of the breach, the restorer of the paths in which to dwell." This verse stayed with me for years. I had written it down in my journal along with a quote from the book where Frangipane referred to these builders saying, *"They will be anointed to gather together His remnant; under that anointing they shall be fruitful and multiply."* Next to this passage I had scribed, Felt God was saying, *"This is why I created you."* I went on to quickly devour the rest of the wisdom expressed in the remaining chapters, completely thrilled with the idea of having gained a better understanding of what my personal call was and my portion amidst the precious remnant called to the work during this glorious time in history. I had learned something new. I was called to help the body become one and to honor one another, but I would do it by rebuilding the ancient ruins, raising up the age-old foundations, repairing the breeches, and restoring the paths to dwell in.

That was five years prior to even thinking about serving leaders in our city. Looking back now, I have to laugh. God certainly isn't ever in a hurry. He is a good Father and, even more important, He is our perfect Father. He knows best how to stoke a good fire. And so often He allows us to sit on a truth for a while, until we get to the point where, like Jeremiah, we say, "I will not mention His word or speak anymore in His name, His word is in my heart like a fire, a fire shut up in my bones, I am weary of holding it in; indeed, I cannot" (Jeremiah 20:9). I used to get frustrated in the times of waiting, but hindsight has taught me to cherish them. Because in the waiting is where He whispers His mysteries to me. In the waiting is where we learn to trust Him. In the waiting is where He forges the character we so desperately need to walk in magnanimous love.

Over the next several years, three friends in ministry and other regional leaders shared separate but confirming words regarding my call to serve leaders. One actually said, "You are called to be a general in God's army!" So, when I read the last definition of magnanimous, I momentarily felt as though time had stopped. I had such clarity of mind and thought. I felt as if God was challenging me to come up higher. Challenging me to love His leaders as He had loved me. I could almost hear a whisper to my heart softly saying, *I have called you to be perfect even as I am perfect. I have called you not only to be a general, but to be a great-hearted general!* In that moment, I knew He was confirming the call on my life to keep leading. Yet at the same time He was saying, *You want to lead and that is a good desire, but I care most not that you lead, but how you lead.* At that point, I had been faithfully following the Lord one step of obedience at a time in ministry for approximately 12 years. I had become well acquainted with the reality that the greater the vision He gave me, the greater the character required of me as I led. The thought was sobering, humbling, and this definition reiterated that I had so much more to learn. All I could do was pray earnestly and ask Him to teach me how to walk in magnanimous love, and then return to the work while I waited and allowed Him to work this magnanimous love deeply into my heart.

# Chapter 3
## COGL'S INCEPTION

I have had the privilege of being a part of the current unity movement in Lansing, Michigan, since its infancy. Every movement has a different flavor. Every city has a different DNA, qualities that are reflective of the kingdom of God and other areas where there is a need for a deep work of God. Our mission has been that "The love of Christ compels us to unite together, as local church and ministry leaders, in order to see the greater Lansing area transformed WITH Christ." Seems like an obvious statement, doesn't it? One that any church in any city should be willing to say "yes" to. But how often do we see churches intentionally look for ways to partner together? I quickly learned that local leaders are often overwhelmed with the daily ins and outs of leading a gathering that includes preaching, teaching, outreach, discipleship, weddings, funerals, and prayer. It became clear if God wanted a consistent and fruitful effort of unified, kingdom-minded Christian leaders that it would require someone to step up who could focus solely on that one purpose. I said, *Here I am, Lord, send me,* only to later realize it would require great personal sacrifice. One that was going to require more of me than I thought I could give in that moment. It would end up being the most painful and, at the same time, the most life-giving endeavor I would ever pursue. Here's how it started.

In 2008, the Lansing unity network was born out of a passion to create a unity movement in the capitol city of Lansing. The city's

Director of Community and Faith-Based Initiatives, Bishop David Maxwell, approached my home church, where I was the Lansing Partnerships Coordinator, to see if we were interested in serving some of the local schools. Since my team was already heavily engaged in helping a local elementary school, I asked if there was any other way we could serve. Bishop Maxwell replied, "Would you be willing to gather the churches and encourage them to serve the community as well?" My boss at the time was a powerhouse of a woman. She was intelligent, powerful, witty, and very driven. I thought for sure since she was sitting in the room that she would want to run with this opportunity. But, she quickly retorted, "Stephanie will." Little did she know God had been stirring my heart regarding unity in the regional body for a few years. I had been waiting and even asking God for just the right moment and wondering when He would open the door to move forward.

## HUMBLE BEGINNINGS

In conjunction with the City of Lansing and the leadership of the church where I served on staff, our first effort to invite pastors to unite in October 2008 resulted in a discussion among a mere eight pastors. Because we were a larger church, we were used to leading large, extravagant events, so eight pastors seemed almost laughable, especially since three of them were from our staff. During the debrief after the meeting, those in senior leadership were disheartened and suggested it wasn't worth pursuing further. But I couldn't let it go. I don't know if it was a gift of divine naiveté or just simple faith, but I knew we had to try again. After all, I knew God said I was made for unity and His ways were going to be beyond anything I could ever dream up on my own. That fateful day when I asked Him what He had created me to do, He gave me the words from 1 Corinthians 1:12-31, challenging me to encourage the church in our city that "God has placed the parts in the body, every one of them, just as He wanted them to be." And also that one part cannot say to the other, "I do not need you!" It didn't make sense, practically speaking, to pour resources into a unity movement made up of a small handful of churches, but God said, *GO!* So I nearly begged for permission and moved forward with the initially unenthusiastic blessing of my church leadership.

Much to everyone's surprise, the movement quickly grew at our second meeting to include more than 30 church leaders. Of course, I was ecstatic. Senior leadership's hope was restored and they gave full support and backing to the gatherings with renewed vigor. My senior pastor and senior director both lent much needed wisdom and sound advice in creating the format of the initial gatherings. I, quite frankly, had no idea how we were going to create unity, but I knew it was time to begin working together. Their recommendation to take a roundtable approach was instrumental in solidifying the foundation upon which we built. Over the course of the next several meetings, we deliberated around the hopes and dreams of those in the room. We answered questions like: *What would we do if we knew we wouldn't fail? What is God calling us to do that we know none of us can accomplish alone? What are some of the greatest needs in our city? And finally, What can we agree upon and who isn't here who should be?*

# LISTENING AND LEARNING

When my senior director asked me what we should call this, there wasn't even a moment's hesitation. I blurted out "The Church of Greater Lansing," now kindly referred to as COGL Network. I tend to be a pretty straight shooter and thought, *Let's not complicate things, just call it what it is.* At the same time, there was also that youthful desire to challenge the deceptive paradigms that propagate the church. One of those paradigms is that the church is the building where congregations gather instead of the people who gather therein. My senior pastor and director shared some concerns regarding the name and the potential for confusion. They eventually agreed it was worth the risk, and the rest is history. Needless to say, the number one concern we heard in the first year was that our network would try to replace the local church through some type of ecumenical gathering. There were moments when I thought, *Why didn't I just listen?* But looking back now, the decision to choose a name that described who we were proved to be an anchor in the years to come and an inspiration for the many who responded to the call.

I spent hundreds of hours in lunch meetings, church gatherings, prayer meetings, and official city meetings, determined to build relationships, to listen to local leaders, and to understand their sincere concerns. We clarified as a group that we would not be a local church in the traditional sense. Instead, we were a network of churches, pastors and Christian leaders in Michigan's Ingham, Eaton and Clinton Counties who were joining forces to help make an indelible spiritual and practical impact on the Lansing Metropolitan area and its communities. We decided to partner with a variety of community organizations, nonprofits, and businesses to pray for and seek the peace and prosperity of our shared community. We defined ourselves as a representation of the Church — with a capital "C." While we were comprised of diverse populations, denominations, ideas and worship styles, we agreed that all participants would be Christian and would be committed to the basic tenants of the Bible.

In response to then-Lansing Mayor Virg Bernero's request that area churches address the hunger issue, more than 35 churches, businesses and entrepreneurs in the public sector came together in early 2009 to raise funds and distribute food to 3,000 families in the Tri-county area. In the following three-year period we led a yearly Food Drop, bringing COGL churches together to raise more than $380,000 to help stomp out hunger locally. It all started with a commitment to put "Love in action." The Church united to meet a practical need by delivering food to hungry families.

We didn't know it at the time, but God was up to something so much bigger. It was during this catalytic event that hearts began to stir and church leaders began to see that we can accomplish so much more for the kingdom of God by working together than we ever could isolated in our organizational silos. The institutional veil was being lifted, and hearts were being awakened to embrace a kingdom vision, something we knew would require us to work together to accomplish.

As COGL continued to develop, we strove to live out our mission statement: "The love of Christ compels us to unite together, as local church and ministry leaders, in order to see the greater Lansing area transformed WITH Christ." We added a learning component, bringing in well-known speakers such as Eric Swanson, Reggie McNeal, Rick Rusaw, Frank Turek, Brenda Salter McNeil, Doug Pollock, and Tony Campolo. Adding the educational element allowed us to grow together through the highest-quality teaching we could provide to regional leaders and Christians. Our hope was to bring in a variety of speakers with assorted affiliations, styles and specialties. As I began to develop relationships with other pastors and Christians in the region, I learned that many of the smaller churches had the passion and people willing to do the sacrificial work of the ministry. Unfortunately, funding was often a struggle for these churches, and it hindered them from bringing in leaders utilizing the most up-to-date tools to equip their people to successfully carry on the work. Their leaders' dreams and desires were just as dynamic as those of the leaders in the larger churches, but because of their willingness to serve believers with lower incomes, they were often constrained by limited budgets. My heart broke for them, and at the same time I developed a deep admiration for their courage, perseverance, and the extravagant love they were displaying toward our city dwellers on a daily basis. Not only were their budgets limited, but these leaders were often working beyond their capacity. The daily ministry demands significantly limited their time to build into their leaders.

As these relationships developed, we began to discuss the possibilities of smaller churches partnering with larger churches. It became very clear we shared the desire to collaborate and that not only would the pastors and leaders benefit from a unified experience but their congregations would as well. These collaborations included putting a roof on an inner-city church, gathering quarterly for unified prayer and worship, and including small church leaders in the larger-church Christmas events. Initially there was some hesitation — what if engaging entire congregations caused families to shift their membership to the larger churches? Instead, those who helped lead these unified events were equipped and sent back to their churches with new skills, allowing them to become vital assets to their home churches! They quickly understood that our intentions were to build the kingdom of God, not any one local church, and they saw how their church families would benefit from our conferences and other unified events. As we hosted the first few events, friendships and connections began to form. There seemed to be an excitement as the leaders and churches in our city actually prioritized Jesus and worked together to transform our city WITH Christ! We were very intentional and prayerful in selecting a group of leaders to plan each event; every team was diverse, representing varied denominations, genders and community passions. This commitment to grow together has been refined over the last eight years, resulting in deep relationships between church leaders and congregants alike. These relationships provide a much-needed peer support system for the leaders and a broader church body experience for believers in the Greater Lansing area.

## LEAVING THE EAGLE'S NEST

In August 2012, the church that housed COGL and helped launch it encouraged COGL to file for 501(c)(3) status. For three years we had been housed at my local church and run by a leadership team I facilitated, and I was sincerely concerned this shift was premature. Still we proceeded with the transition to become a 501(c)(3) organization.

Much to my dismay, I was noticing a pattern of increasing disengagement from our local body starting in 2010. At the time, our board consisted of representatives from five churches, led by Walter Gibson, dear friend, pastor of Pilgrim Rest Baptist Church and the 2012 COGL Board President. The board gathered regularly to determine COGL's future direction and values. Though I had doubts about the timing of the move to become a nonprofit organization, Apostle Wendy Waterson of Sanctuary Gate Church and one-time COGL Board Secretary, reflected positively on the timing. As she said, "Moving to a formal non-profit marked a maturing of the ministry. It welcomed the participation of other pastors and leaders outside the original founding group. It made it a Body-of-Christ ministry rather than something for just a few. Other pastors and Christian leaders can now contribute equally to the vision and leadership of the ministry."

After much prayer and wrestling with God as the ministry transitioned out of our local church and into the community, I accepted the position the board offered me, becoming the executive director of the new 501(c)(3) organization in September 2012. The board was very excited about this shift, but I honestly cannot say I shared their enthusiasm. I was suddenly thrust out from the safety and resources my home church offered. I also found myself shifting out of a leadership role that allowed me to lead the board meetings, decide how to accomplish our goals, and function as the quasi-president of the movement; my new role made me an administrator without any voting rights. With no paid clerical support, I suddenly was given all of the administrative responsibilities of the new organization. Administration is not my gift, so this new role felt like a burden to me. I found myself administrating for a board of pastors after spending the last three years convincing them that unity was something worth pursuing. After three years of vision casting and building a relational network, it felt like a setback. I was suddenly in a position where the original vision I was excited about was being handed to others to fulfill, and it felt like this shift would result in the inevitable death of my destiny.

Little did I know then that this was actually the pathway to *finding* my destiny. God was dealing with my pride and testing my willingness to trust Him to work through others. Quite frankly, I felt like I had been demoted. The change would greatly restrict my ability to direct, lead and facilitate the board as I had in the formative years leading up to the transition. It took hours of prayer, repentance and forgiveness to make the shift to my new position with a right heart.

When I was wrestling with God about the whole transition and boldly stating my case before Him, He prompted my spirit with a simple question, *Will you love them?* I felt a bit like the woman in 1 Kings 3:23 who was arguing with the other mother that a living child was hers when suddenly King Solomon said, "Bring me a sword." He then gave an order: "Cut the living child in two, and give half to one and half to the other." Imagine with me the heart of the parent in that brief moment. She had a split second to choose — the death of the son she loved so much or the painful potential of knowing he would live but not being able to see him grow into a young man. At that moment, I was initially crushed. I realized that if I really loved God and if He had called me to this and He wanted this, then it didn't matter what happened to me or what my position in our local body would be. It didn't matter how long it would take to accomplish the goal. It didn't matter what people would say. It didn't matter if I ever got paid. He was worth it, whatever the cost! I had been asking these leaders to walk in love, to trust one another, to be courageous — and now it was my turn. I had to trust that God could speak to and through this board without my influence. I had to trust God's timing. And, I had to humble myself and trust that if Abba had another plan it was only a matter of time before He would put things back into kingdom order. The lessons I learned during the next two and a half years in an administrative, non-decision-making role formed in me the very character I would need to see the realization of the vision God had given.

## INITIAL INTEREST AND GROWTH

By 2013, more than 165 churches and 25 local businesses were participating in COGL. Separating from the local body proved to the community that we were serious about the regional Church's ownership of our movement. While these numbers were encouraging, there was so much more to do. There were still approximately 300 churches in Lansing who were not yet part of COGL but who could benefit from becoming partners. I was passionate about the impact COGL could have to "Seek the peace and prosperity of the city to which I have sent you" (Jeremiah 29:7). I continued to meet monthly with countless leaders and encouraged more churches to join COGL and be part of the collaborative approach God was developing to transform Lansing. I knew COGL was an expression of God's highest love. When the body of Christ humbly gathers together to seek God's best for each other and those God has placed in their region, it's a beautiful thing to watch. It testifies to His goodness. It draws the lost to Christ!

According to Trinity Church's then Lead Pastor Phil Posthuma, there were several reasons churches should consider the mission of COGL. He said, "If COGL ceased to exist today, there is no other entity in the city that draws pastors together to create bonds of friendship across ethnic lines. There is no other entity that pulls churches across the city together to serve the city in the name of Christ. We still have a lot to learn from each other and a lot of love to share across church leaders."

Bishop David Maxwell from Eliezer Temple Church, who was also a COGL board member, emphasized that COGL is instrumental because it has "demonstrated that two sectors of our society — the public sector as well as the faith community — can collaborate together for the common goal of helping people. This has opened the door for God to honor that behavior and pour out blessings on our region because we are in line with His word."

Over the first two years as a 501(c)(3), God doubled the number of churches participating. He was up to something wonderful and we were excited to be a part of it! By the end of 2013, COGL had endured a lot of changes, but we praised God that we were flourishing despite the transitions. We pressed in and pilgrimaged on, knowing God was doing something amazing and believing it was well worth the risk involved to be a part of it.

# Chapter 4
## JUST KILL ME ALREADY

Like me, you may be laughing as you read the title of this chapter, but I'm going to share a few more details about the real struggle I had shifting out of the comfort of my church into the competitive world of a 501(c)(3) ministry. So often when discussing ministry, we like to keep it neat and clean — and many times with good reason. There are those who will always misinterpret what we are saying, as they did with the apostles, but that does not mean we shouldn't share the truth. According to Peter, the Apostle Paul was misunderstood. In 2 Peter 3:16 he tells us this about Paul, "He writes the same way in all his letters, speaking in them of these matters. His letters contain some things that are hard to understand, which ignorant and unstable people distort, as they do the other Scriptures, to their own destruction." That will always be the case when we are dealing with broken people and people who do not know the love of God.

However, a lack of transparency about the very real battle being waged as we work out our salvation with fear and trembling can be detrimental to the next generation of believers. While I do agree that it is important to protect the reputations of those we are in relationship with and to carefully tell a story that honors others, I have also learned it is dangerous to cover a matter so that it shrouds the realities of the fundamental battle waged to gain victory in Christ! If we are not careful, we can inadvertently give the impression that our journey with God has been free from troubles, hardships, and crossroads, which is rarely the case. Our willingness to be transparent about our own personal struggles better equips the upcoming generations to persevere into their promised land.

My hope is that sharing these details will do just that for you. Looking back now, I have to laugh, because it all worked out. However, in that moment of transition the fears and feelings I'm about to share with you were no laughing matter. When sharing the details of our struggles, we should use wisdom for sure, but the power and grace of God are fully appreciated when we reveal the very real struggle each of us faces as we choose to die that Christ may live.

The beauty of this glorious battle is that we are not alone as we stand, both flawed and faithful, in service to Father God. We are surrounded by a great cloud of witnesses who were also far from perfect and yet were powerful men and women in partnership with the King of kings. It's imperative that we follow the leading of the Holy Spirit who penned the Scriptures and painted a very candid picture of the patriarchs of our faith. Abraham lied, or at least told a half-truth, about his wife Sarah being his sister, basically offering her to a king to protect himself. Sarah, the mother of Isaac, laughed at God and then lied about it to His face! Jacob cheated his brother out of his inheritance. Moses got angry with God's people and dishonored God in the sight of His people. Rahab was a prostitute. David committed adultery with Bathsheba and then murdered her husband to cover it up. Euodia and Syntyche had such a strong disagreement that Paul wrote a letter to ask a friend to help them work it out.

So we are in good company! It is important that we all come before our Lord with unveiled faces. As we become more like Christ and grow in divine love, we realize that we only become like him to the measure we are willing to admit we have further to go and need His help. Second Corinthians 3:18 says, "And we all, who with *unveiled faces* contemplate the Lord's glory, *are being transformed* into His image with ever-increasing glory, which comes from the Lord, who is the Spirit" (emphasis mine). Hereafter, though I won't give too much detail in an attempt to honor others, I will be very honest about my internal conversation in hopes that you will be encouraged to be more transparent with the Lord and with those you lead. The Scripture above says it is when we unveil our faces that we are transformed into His image with ever-increasing glory. God gets all the glory when people know about us what we know about ourselves!

## WHEN, GOD, WHEN?

In 2005, when we arrived at our church, I had just finished writing and directing a play with a dear friend and felt led to turn down a ministry position offered to me at her church at that time. I had also recently stepped down as assistant director of the local women's shelter. I was full of zeal for Jesus and wanted to serve somewhere, but my children were still quite young and God had made it very clear that they were to be my sole ministry for a season. I am so thankful for the grace He gave me to heed His directive. Today we are still seeing the fruit of it in our children's lives. They are healthy, whole-hearted, passionate followers of Jesus who are an absolute delight to my husband and me.

I was still preaching at the local jail once a month, but everything else had come to a screeching halt. I felt like my professional ministry track was on pause, but I continued to pray and ask the Lord for the green light, hopeful that He would soon release me to do ministry in the church again. At that time, I had gained a lot of knowledge but hadn't persevered long enough to bear the fruit of patience quite yet! I wanted God to move and nothing seemed to be moving fast enough for me. I spent an entire year waiting, serving in the children's ministry, and praying before my prayer was answered. The thought I battled the most was, *When, God, when?* I remember praying something like this: *Father, I know I am impatient and Your timing and will are perfect. Please forgive me for being impatient. I know You have asked me to wait and I am willing, but please don't let me miss Your opportunities. If it's time now, have someone ask me to volunteer and I will do whatever You put before me.*

As the year continued, I became increasingly content serving my family and had learned to be still ... well, sort of. Then the opportunity finally came. A woman by the name of Anne approached me out of the blue and said, "I heard you used to do ministry with Lisa at the women's shelter. I was asking her about volunteer leaders and she told me you were attending our church." I was so thankful to have been released by the Lord to serve in the church that they could have asked me to clean toilets and I would have said yes! Her ask was quite simple. They needed a leader for their Thanksgiving basket ministry. Little did I realize this seemingly insignificant start was the onramp to my destiny. I was convinced whatever door opened would lead me to the first step in doing what God had called me to do: unify.

As I coordinated that ministry, I learned quickly how much I hated administrative work. I am not a detail person. I can do vision and broad-stroke brainstorming sessions for 48 hours straight, but if you give me a list of volunteer names and addresses to organize, you're asking for trouble. The numbers will start to blur and my brain becomes so overwhelmed at the details in front of me that I become almost paralyzed. I will never be the type of person who can sit down and enjoy organizing details or managing large chunks of data. The small details that administratively gifted individuals thrive on often overwhelm me. I can think of many things worse than death, and managing details is definitely one of them. Ha!

I admire my husband; he is a fantastic detail guy. He loves the order and the organizational aspects of his job and, needless to say, he helped me a lot that first year. I grew to deeply appreciate those around me who were administrative. When joining a ministry, I was able to focus on reorganizing their processes and create biblically based vision and mission statements, but after accomplishing those tasks I was bored. New team leaders would be found and I would move on to something new.

I loved the leaders I had met so far at the church and had a desire to come on staff and help build God's kingdom. In 2008, Sharina, the director of Outreach, called me and asked me to pray about coming on staff as the onsite ministries coordinator for the church, which was then a 3,500-member church. Little did she know I had been praying for God to open a door for me to be formally hired if this was His will for me. So, my answer to her when she asked me to pray was, "I don't need to — this is an answer to prayer." She wisely asked me to take a few days, pray about it, discuss it with my husband, and get back with her. I did, and my husband, Shane, gave his blessing.

# THE NITTY GRITTY

At that time, I thought I had arrived in the job of my dreams. I was so excited. I was finally doing God's work professionally. It was important, it was meaningful, and I was helping the leaders as they changed people's lives. My direct bosses seemed to genuinely take interest in me and to sincerely want me to grow and become all God had called me to be. By then, I had learned a lot about the importance of details and by the grace of God grew in my ability to be a better steward of them — or, so I thought. I worked for a precious man of God, whom I still deeply respect to this day, but he once edited a single brochure for a two-day event 19 times. I literally thought, "Lord, just kill me already. How many times can I change this and still not have it right? How many people are we going to get opinions from to try and make it just right? For the love of God, would someone just make a decision?!"

As with any job, the honeymoon period lasted about a year and then the real work began. If I were going to learn to work well with others, I became painfully aware that I needed to learn to work at a much slower pace, or at least grow in grace toward those who moved slower than I did.

It was about then that I was approached by Bishop Maxwell, from the city of Lansing, my now dear friend, asking me to unite the pastors. As I shared earlier, this was something I was born for. It was tied to the word God had given me about my purpose: to bring unity. As the years passed, my role in the local body seemed less and less interesting, and creating this network consumed me. It was the only thing I found pleasure in doing; all the other internal assignments at the church just lost their appeal. I didn't feel challenged by them. They didn't excite me at all, and, quite frankly, I had found others who could lead those initiatives better than I could. I had hoped to be able to convince my leadership that the unity movement would benefit the church at large. I could see how it could have positioned the organization to be a leader in the region, but they just didn't seem interested. Our lead pastor at the time had finished the book *Simple Church* by Thom Rainer and Eric Geiger and was convinced that pairing down the ministries in the church to a few focused efforts was the best way to go. I was convinced COGL would and should make the cut, but as things moved forward it became increasingly obvious he had different plans. This is where it got messy.

Quite frankly, I didn't want to leave the comfort of my home church. I had everything I could ever need. Access to people, resources, offices, rooms, amenities, and the funding needed to run the entire organization. I felt safe, secure and supported, so when our leadership first presented the idea of moving COGL to a 501(c)(3) organization I thought they must be joking. First, why would they want to do that, given the magnitude of the vision; and, second, why would they throw this baby out to the wolves to figure out life on her own? As I was the baby in this scenario, you can see the self-centeredness of my thought process, but I was dead serious. I thought they were trying to kill this beautiful thing God has just birthed through me.

Then the fateful day came. I could no longer pretend like the transition wasn't a possibility. My direct boss, whom I deeply admire, called me into his office and said, "Stephanie, if I were to ask you today to choose either COGL or the position of director for local outreach, which would you choose?" I couldn't give him an answer that day. I asked if I could pray about it and I did. The church was my home, my family, my friends and the place where I had learned so much. I was honored at the thought that I could potentially be a director, the highest level of leadership offered to a staffer aside from the pastoral roles. Everything in my flesh wanted to say "yes." I thought *What a life! I could work with my friends, have great pay and benefits. Life would be a blast and I could remain here in this place I've grown to love so much. I found myself asking God, If this is from You, Lord, please say yes! What an honor, what a blessing. Surely this must be You.*

However, the more I prayed, the less I had peace about remaining on staff. When I thought about continuing with COGL, I realized a transition of COGL out into the community was the preferred direction of the leadership. It had become clear this shift was inevitable, and, yet, God was asking me to take this position. I knew it would be a hard road ahead, with less support and full of unknowns. I knew it meant I would have to go it alone with God and that I would likely receive less and less input from this family I had grown to love so much. I would have to take some serious risks to see COGL flourish. I wouldn't have health insurance benefits, I wouldn't be secure, safe, or amidst friends. In fact, in some ways just the opposite was proving to be true. I felt so ill-equipped and I was scared of failing. I looked at everything that had transpired over the course of my ministry career and thought, *Lord, I can't do this. I'm not ready. Where do I even start?* I remembered how much I hated the administrative aspect of my job and thought this would have to be God for me to say yes.

The more I prayed, the more uneasy I felt, because it was becoming clear that my call was to remain with COGL. My home church was making it unmistakably known that the leadership of COGL would be shifting out of my comfort zone. When I returned to my boss and shared what I felt God was saying, I think he was shocked. I was holding fast to every promise I had about God's character and goodness because I had a word about being created for unity and being called as a general. Everything seemed so intimidating in those moments. I can remember when the leadership had shared the decision to transition COGL to a 501(c)(3); I had gone home and wept. I felt like a soldier being sent out on a mission that might or might not go well, but was of no concern to the commanders. I am not saying that this was the heart of the leaders I served; I'm simply saying that it was how I felt in that moment.

## KEEP MOVING FORWARD

I found as the transition progressed and the Simple Church changes were taking place in the organization, it became more and more difficult to talk with my friends and colleagues about the situation and get an honest response. At that time, the new director of outreach had been hired, so I was relegated to an old lost-and-found closet for my office. It literally had a sign above it that said, "Lost and Found." I can remember walking into the office one day and asking God under my breath, *Really, the lost and found closet. Father, why?* I heard Him respond, *I send them in lost and you send them out found.* Father God is so kind and has a wonderful sense of humor. I never had a problem with my new office after that conversation. In that season of transitions, many of my co-workers were struggling as well with their own ministry futures, wondering whether they would survive the cuts. They simply didn't have the capacity to console, comfort or encourage me, so I reached out to a coach and friend, Glenn Barth.

Glenn is with Good Cities in Eden Prairie, Minnesota. He works with leaders of city-based movements across the nation. He encouraged me to share with my leadership that the model in which a single congregation backs a new movement was the most sustainable model to date. When non-profit organizations launch outside the church, they often face funding problems and struggle to survive. That bit of information wasn't exactly helping my comfort level! I said to him that day, "Glenn I don't know what to do. I feel like I am being squeezed out, and I have nowhere to go — no building, no volunteers, no support, all the responsibility and no authority." I had just learned that as the soon-to-be executive director, I would have no voting rights on the board of directors. I asked Glenn, "What do I do?" He said something to me that day that I will never forget, "Stephanie, just keep moving forward. Do you remember what God said when all the people of Israel were standing at the Jordan about to cross into their promised land? He told them to simply move forward."

I had absolutely no desire to do this in my own strength, and more than ever I needed a directive straight from the heart of Father God. The risk was huge, the road ahead looked treacherous, and I didn't want to fight any unnecessary battles. Later that week, I turned my Bible to Exodus 14 and began to read. I asked God to whisper to me once again. As I started at verse one and continued reading through the chapter, I could relate to Moses and the Israelites. I felt as if I were leaving the land where everything was provided for me, but I had also worked under a hard task master, at least for those last couple of years. The entire staff was groaning under the pressure of the unknown, the potential that their ministries might also be cut, and were also feeling fearful. It was truly a test of our character in Christ. Would we trust God and hold fast to His promises for us, resting in His goodness and grace, and knowing He had good plans to prosper us and not to harm us?

I confess I wavered in that moment. I was tempted to shed light on some things I had experienced that could have brought the entire process to a screeching halt, but I felt convicted that the Lord said to let it go and instead choose love, choose mercy, choose to trust Him. So I did. As I look back on that season of my journey, it was a path abounding with opportunities to love magnanimously. I literally at times felt as though I was dying. My flesh certainly was, and that was a good thing. If God was going to use me to change a city, there wouldn't be any room for my flesh to remain a priority. Little did I know then that this was just the beginning of my crash course on how to die daily and pick up my cross and follow Jesus.

As I continued reading in Exodus 14, I came to verse 13, "Moses answered the people, 'Do not be afraid. Stand firm and you will see the deliverance the Lord will bring you today. The Egyptians you see today you will never see again. The Lord will fight for you; you need only to be still.'" After reading these words, I began to weep. The pressures of the daily unknown and the hoping that this was all a bad dream began to overwhelm me. Although I knew I was safe in His arms and that He would rescue me, I proceeded to tell Him how afraid I was and ask if He was sure this was the right decision?

As I wiped my tears and blew my nose, my eyesight cleared up enough to see Exodus 14:15, "Then the Lord said to Moses, 'Why are you crying out to me? Tell the Israelites to move on. Raise your staff and stretch out your hand over the sea to divide the water so that the Israelites can go through the sea on dry ground. I will harden the hearts of the Egyptians so that they will go in after them. And I will gain glory through Pharaoh and all his army, through his chariots and his horsemen. The Egyptians will know that I am the Lord when I gain glory through Pharaoh, his chariots and his horsemen.'" I was shocked and sobered by the reality that God was rebuking me. The words "Why are you crying out to me? Tell the Israelites to move on!" jumped off the page and struck my heart with great conviction. In that moment, I realized I had been at a crisis of faith. The fears, concerns and pressures seemed insignificant in comparison to the greatness of our God. Then my eyes fell down the page a bit further to "Raise your staff and stretch out your hand." It was as if in that moment God was saying, *Stephanie, what is in your hand? Go forward with what I have already given you: the relationships, the vision, the events, and go in faith! I have given you everything you need to do what I have asked of you.* In other words, He was saying to move forward, hold onto what had been successful, and tell the people to march on! Much like Moses' conversation with God in the dessert at the burning bush (Exodus 4:2), I was arguing with God, telling Him, *But I am not schooled, I have no degree, and they don't even want to follow me.* Those two simple words, "Move on!" were the words I needed to hear. They filled my heart with the courage to take that next step, with or without the support of the huge organization I had grown to love and with or without all the support to which I was accustomed.

I can still vividly remember the day I was asked to choose either to continue to work with COGL Network for free and also work an additional 20 hours in another department, or to leave the staff entirely and work only for the network. I felt so dishonored, dismayed and alone. With the call to home-school our children, there was no way I could do both. In that moment I knew what I needed to do. I couldn't put it off any longer. It was time. I packed up my boxes, my files, and my personal belongings. After shedding a few tears, I wrote a short email to my colleagues thanking them for the honor of having worked with them and asking them to pray for me as I moved forward. Then I headed out to set up my home office. All the way home I was praying, *Lord, I have done as You asked. Lead me on.*

Over the course of the seven years I was on staff at this church, I was asked to help with more than 10 different ministries that were either struggling or stuck, or with new ministries in the organization. Again and again, when given a new assignment I would assess, clarify the vision, design systems, and recommend leaders to carry it out and share the information with the current leadership team. Looking back, I now realize God had prepared me in His own way. He had truly given me everything I needed to succeed.

# Chapter 5
## I AM NO MAN

We Americans love a good story. I especially love an action-packed heroic movie, one that has believable characters who possess human vulnerabilities and weaknesses. I tend to lean toward films where the battle is seemingly impossible to win but the uncompromising character of the underdog unexpectedly triumphs over the vicious villain. There is something divine about those story lines. They give hope to the soul, encouragement to the heart, faith to a fear-filled mind, and strength to the weary warrior. I am not an avid sports fan nor do I have any particular hobbies outside of ministry and doing daily life, but I often enjoy a good motion picture, especially when I am feeling ministry-weary. Since I'm a woman, I love it when a female heroine displays great courage and leadership, resulting in an unexpected victory.

One of my favorite scenes is from a movie series called The *Lord of the Rings Trilogy*. In *Return of the King* there is an ongoing battle for peace in Middle-earth led by Aragorn, the chosen one, who has an uncanny resemblance to Jesus. Sounds like a familiar battle being waged here on earth, right? This trilogy has a plethora of prophetic parallels if one is looking for them. They are not perfect parallels by any means but undeniable parallels nonetheless. At one point in this motion picture, Eowyn, a noble woman of Rohan, is asked, "What do you fear, my lady?" She replies, "A cage, to stay behind bars until use and old age accept them, and all chance of great deeds is gone beyond recall or desire." This noble woman longed to fight against the wicked Witch-king at the battle of the Pelennor Fields. She couldn't bear the thought of being relegated to the typical path for a woman of her time. For her it would be comparable to being a wild bird meant to fly free but instead locked up in a confining cage. Her heart longed to be on the front lines fighting with the strongest warriors in the land, but she'd been told to go home by the male soldiers suiting up for war. After a sobering assessment of the consequences, she had a decision to make. She could retreat and concede that she wasn't fit for battle, or she could move forward and valiantly live out her destiny. In the brazen spirit of a bold-hearted fighter — and unknown to the men — she chose to suit up with the men and march alongside the soldiers into combat despite their objections.

At the climax of the Pelennor Fields battle, Eowyn comes face to face with the evil Witch-king of Angmar. He grabs her by the throat and says, "You fool. No man can kill me. Die now!" The Witch-king is then caught off guard by another solider striking him from behind. He releases Eowyn and she falls to the ground. After a dramatic pause, Eowyn climbs to her feet with confidence as if she now realizes her purpose as a woman. She removes her helmet, resolutely looks the Witch-king in the face, and says, "I am no man." Then she plunges her sword into the darkness that is his being, winning the battle for all of Middle-earth. The first time I saw that scene I just about jumped out of my chair. I thought, *Yes! Evil destroyed, death itself conquered — that is how I want to live for my King, Jesus!*

# HINDSIGHT IS 20/20

I have always been a bit of a warrior at heart myself. As strange as it sounds, even in my young teenage years I had an unshakable inclination toward justice. I longed to see justice served, wrongs righted, the poor uplifted, the hurting healed, the hopeless encouraged and the bullied defended. I can remember one instance like it was yesterday. My little brother had been playing football down the street with some of the boys in the neighborhood. Sean was always a wiry kid. He was small in size but what he lacked in stature he made up for with his quick-witted humor, which often got him into trouble. That day I was at the house doing chores when someone rushed in and told me the neighborhood boys were ganging up on my little brother. My mom worked a full-time job and I had taken it upon myself to ensure my siblings were protected and cared for while she was gone. On getting this news of a budding brawl, I was instantly filled with righteous indignation. My head was full of questions. *Who do they think they are? Why can't they pick on someone their own size?* And finally, *How can they think they will get away with this?*

They were playing in a field about two blocks from my house. I had my shoes on and was out the door in under 60 seconds flat. In a full-on sprint I arrived at the field completely out of breath and ready to defend my little brother. I thought *Surely they can see he is small and has no chance of defending himself against all of them. Well, I can even these odds a bit.*

In those early teen years, I still had a physical advantage over most of the boys my age. As I ran up to the field, I can remember one boy saying, "Guys, guys, stop. Stephanie's here." Before they could say a word, I blurted out, "Why don't you pick on someone your own size?" The boys looked up and saw me. Their eyes widened, and they backed away from my little brother, who was now curled up on the ground trying to protect himself. I can still remember the fear on those boys' faces when they saw me. I have no idea what my facial expression looked like, but my siblings still tease me about it to this day, more than 30 years later. Apparently, my expression clearly communicated that I would stop at nothing to protect Sean.

This sense of justice has tempered a bit as I have grown older but it has never completely gone away. The misguided zeal of my youth has merely been redirected at the enemies of our souls, Satan and his cohorts. I have learned that in Christ, "Our struggle is not against flesh and blood, but against the rulers, against the authorities, against the powers of this dark world and against the spiritual forces of evil in the heavenly realms" (Ephesians 6:12).

Just before I packed my boxes to "move forward" with COGL, a senior leader shared with me that two local pastors had approached him with serious concerns about the fact that I was a woman. One actually had requested that I be removed from a leadership position altogether. I was so thankful to learn that my pastor had defended my call to lead and informed them that there wasn't any biblical foundation for suggesting that a woman couldn't lead outside the church.

I can remember praising God with a good friend in my office while tears streamed down my face, trying to imagine how the Lord was going to work it all out. She and her husband would later become my Aaron and Hur (Exodus 17:12). Many times in the two years following, they held up my arms in prayer while a war was being waged.

I have no doubt their faithfulness and prayers are two of the reasons COGL exists today. Looking back now I can see how God positioned that leader in my life during that season to protect me from nascent persecution. In hindsight, the painful shift to a non-voting executive director role actually protected me and allowed me to continue to create the systems and build the relationships essential to seeing the vision fulfilled. What I had perceived as persecution and hardship God had worked together for my good! Ultimately the enemy pulled out all the stops. He couldn't get me to disobey, he couldn't get me to be paralyzed by fear, he couldn't convince me to quit and give up, so he attacked the one thing I couldn't change — the fact that I was a woman.

You may find it surprising to know that I once believed it wasn't possible, probable, nor a promise to be considered that I, a mere woman, should, could, or would be called to lead. In fact, I actually struggled with the call to lead for several years. I would like to humbly propose that the Scriptures do demonstrate that both men and women are called to lead, to serve, to love and to do great exploits in the name of God, our Father! I specifically struggled with the problematic verses most often cited to negate the validity of female leaders: 1 Corinthians 14:34 and 1 Timothy 2:12. The matter was only settled in my heart after a more in-depth study helped me contextualize those verses in their perspective chapters, books and cultural settings. It took me several years of prayerful examination to finally gain the peace I needed to move forward in my personal call to lead. While I do understand the sincere desire of so many to honor God, obey His Word, and maintain kingdom order, there is a very real struggle the church is facing and needs to resolve about women and their leadership in the church.

I recognize this small paragraph cannot satisfy the church's need for a full dissertation on the validity of God's call on women to lead in the church. However, I would be remiss if I, a female leader, did not at least challenge you to prayerfully examine a few biblical examples of female leaders. I humbly submit a few scriptural contradictions to the long-held belief that women cannot or should not be allowed to lead. In the Garden of Eden prior to the fall of man, God blessed Adam and Eve and *commanded them both* to subdue the earth, to rule and to reign (Genesis 1:28). Deborah was a prophet who led all of Israel under the old covenant (Judges 4:4). Junia was a female whom Paul said was outstanding among the apostles (Romans 16:7). Anna was a prophet in the temple who declared the redemption of Jerusalem over the infant Christ (Luke 2:36). The Woman at the Well was an evangelist (John 4:1-39). The Chosen Lady was a pastor who received a personal letter from the Apostle John about her church and her children in the Lord (2 John 1). Finally, Priscilla was a teacher and the wife of Aquila; together, she and her husband taught Apollos the way of God more accurately (Acts 18:26). If you are thinking that's not enough to prove my point, you are correct! However, I hope it piqued your interest enough to consider taking a deeper look. Here are a few books that provide a more in-depth look at the issue of women leading in the church: *I Suffer Not a Women: Rethinking I Timothy 2:11-15 in Light of Ancient Evidence* by Richard Clark Kroeger & Catherine Kroeger; *Why Not Women?* by Loren Cunningham; *Women in the Church — A Biblical Theology of Women in Ministry* by Stanley J. Grenz; *Fashioned to Reign* by

Kris Vallotton; *How I Changed My Mind About Women in Leadership*, edited by Alan F. Johnson & Dallas Willard; *10 Lies the Church Tells Women* by Lee Grady; and *What Paul Really Said About Women* by John T. Bristow.

Worldwide we are facing unfathomable levels of Christian persecution, unthinkable acts of rebellion, hatred, self-centeredness and increasingly powerful dark spiritual forces. We are facing a culture committed to flagrant abominations that were once considered taboo but are now openly celebrated. We are seeing brazen acts of injustice, murder, theft, usury, and intentional political manipulations and deceptions. While many of these are age-old tactics of the Devil to divide, deceive and destroy, the outright celebration is most concerning. With such an offensive against truth and righteousness, we need all the warriors we can get and women happen to make up 49.6 percent of the American population. If we do not get this straightened out, half of our soldiers will remain on the sidelines.

Magnanimous love is still the answer to this hurting world, and I would suggest to you that women are well practiced at it. I would also humbly submit that the historical and hierarchical leadership structures provide only a portion of the systemic approaches needed to advance the kingdom of God in this season. While they work well in the local body, a unified movement requires a multi-faceted leadership approach spearheaded by servant leaders who provide structure and order but allow each leader to flourish, lead and contribute to the overall vision. The most successful movements tend to be those that focus less on who is leading and embrace instead a coaching model that helps partner leaders discover their own roles in the movement. The structure must be one that promotes mutual submission, honor and a culture of grace. Women are adept at servant leadership, honoring others, maintaining order, multi-tasking and fiercely protecting those they love. I believe if we want to see the church united and cities and nations discipled, it will take an army of both female and male leaders to make it happen. There is still only one thing that never fails and that's love (1 Corinthians 13:8).

Love fully manifest is quite literally "Christ in you, the hope of glory" (Colossians 1:27). We can only change the world and love others to the measure that we've allowed Christ to be formed in us. Every person who has ever been married understands the reality that a spouse's input and partnership is invaluable. I believe wholeheartedly that while our current season may very well be the most historically difficult to evangelize, it undoubtedly will also be the most fruitful. If we can serve side by side as men and women of God and fight this good fight of faith together, the kingdom of God can be advanced expediently. There are places women can reach that men cannot. There are strengths both men and women have that their counterparts do not possess. I humbly submit that this issue with women in leadership is one that must be resolved if the church desires to truly manifest the fullness of Christ to this hurting world. The Scriptures state that both women and men are heirs to the promise: "So in Christ Jesus you are *all* children of God through faith, for all of you who were baptized into Christ have clothed yourselves with Christ. There is neither Jew nor Gentile, neither slave nor free, *nor is there male and female, for you are all one in Christ Jesus.* If you belong to Christ, then you are Abraham's seed, and heirs according to the promise" (Galatians 3:26-29; emphasis mine). Is it not written in Genesis 1:27 that "God created mankind in His own image, in the image of God he created them; male and female He created them"? This verse specifically addresses the validity that women and men are made in the image of God. It suggests that both the representation of both the male and the female are required to express the fullness of the image of God to the world. Jesus said in John 10:35 that the Scriptures cannot be broken or set aside. It is reasonable therefore to conclude that the full image of God expressed through Christ can only be experienced when both male and female leaders are free to live out the fullness of all that Christ has called, compelled and created them to be. Transforming our cities WITH Christ will require men and women to listen, lead and love magnanimously.

# Chapter 6
## THE AMERICAN DREAM

In 2015, a good friend forwarded an email to me about a vision a young man named Justin had shared at his church. It was so relevant to how COGL functions and what I believe God wants to say to the cooperate church today that I simply had to share it here. The precepts it reveals are absolutely vital to ensuring the American Church thrives in this generation and those to come. Justin Reid, a friend from House of Prayer East Lansing, formerly The Furnace, writes:

*I was in a room with the Lord and there was a table between us. On the table there was a diagram of the electrical grid for a city. It was a glowing rectangle with lines going vertically and horizontally. I asked the Lord what it was and he said it was made up of the people of God in a city. Each of the segments in the grid represented different churches in the city. He showed me that for the grid to work properly and for the power to get to every part of the city, each of the segments (the churches) needed to be connected to the power source (Christ) as well as to each other. It was clear that if any of the segments weren't connected to the others, then that part of the city would go without power. I felt like God was showing me that, in a sense, any church can be individually connected to God and that His power can be at work in them, but that the 'power grid' God has designed is one where the churches are connected to one another. The things God desires to do in a city (His power at work) cannot happen unless the churches are connected to one another.*

As I was reading this email for the first time in the spring of 2015, my spirit resounded with an enthusiastic *Amen!* Repeatedly over the years, COGL has challenged leaders with the beautiful truth and promise of the bestowed blessing stated in Psalm 133: "How good and pleasant it is when God's people live together in unity! It is like precious oil poured on the head, running down on the beard, running down on Aaron's beard, down on the collar of his robe. It is as if the dew of Hermon were falling on Mount Zion. For there the Lord bestows his blessing, even life forevermore." Justin's experience in prayer that day confirmed the blessing kingdom leaders in Lansing were experiencing as we simply connected WITH other Christians who shared common passions and a fervent love for Jesus. It is my strong conviction that magnanimous love can only be tested in the context of community and that is best proven in the context of a connected group of individuals who have different preferences, passions and intrinsic doctrines. Dennis Moore and Scott Rolff, with Ministry Coaching Making Disciples (MCMD), were instrumental in helping us purposefully build the high-trust relationships necessary to remain connected long term. Doing ministry WITH other ministries and WITH Christ quickly became one of our core values, so much so that we have intentionally capitalized it in our tagline "United to Transform Cities WITH Christ!" in an effort to keep it constantly before our hearts. For us, WITH Christ came to mean we were not doing the work in our own strength but in Christ's strength and that meant we needed to work WITH others if we wanted to represent Christ fully to our city!

For me personally, Justin's experience helped me see plainly how God was using me in the city to ensure that connectivity was maintained and encouraged between kingdom leaders. As president of COGL Network, I basically serve kingdom leaders in our region to ensure and maintain spiritual connections. It even clarified for me God's divine providence over my husband's job as a supervisor of distribution for water and light. Shane literally oversees our city's entire electrical grid on a daily basis, ensuring physical light reaches our city and beyond. I am in awe that God arranged the perfect prophetic parallel in our separate vocations. These seemingly insignificant details paint a beautiful picture of God's grace in our lives. Only God could have known such things, only He would take care to weave even this finest detail into His perfect plan.

# PLUG IN

As privileged citizens of the United States of America, we often cling to the American Dream that an individual can make a way, cultivate an idea, envision the impossible and make it a reality all by oneself. But the truth is we can't. It takes consumers willing to purchase our products, partners willing to do their portion, friends open to sharing our ideas, and an invested few willing to take the risk and do the hard work, persevering until the dream is realized. Wikipedia defines the American Dream as, "A set of ideals in which freedom includes the opportunity for prosperity and success, as well as an often upward social mobility for the family and children, achieved through hard work in a society said to have few barriers."

Over the last decade, I've had the privilege of working with more than 210 regional church leaders, most of whom are sacrificially living for Christ. While it is a rare occasion, it still surprises me when a pulpiteer clings to the American Dream mantra as the end game for believers, as if prosperity, success and upward social mobility definitively describe a Christian life, organization or church that has "arrived!" Anyone who has worked in the church knows that one must be fluent in politics to navigate and survive some church cultures. Is it possible in these cases that our red, white and blue bleeding hearts have tainted the fabric of our church DNA so much so that we have become more concerned about the upward mobility of our own kingdoms — our congregational numbers, our buildings, our personal ministries, or even our next book or promotion — at the expense of expanding the kingdom of God? Though they are uncommon occurrences, it does grieve my heart and I believe it grieves God's heart as well when we have taken the very thing that we have freely received and peddle it for the purpose of personal profit in contrast to offering it to the body of Christ to build them up. These are matters of the heart, matters only God can weigh upon the scales of His perfect justice. Building His kingdom is not for the purpose of the financial prosperity of our own personal ministries, but for the spiritual prospering of the body of Christ. As leaders we must be so careful to keep it all about Jesus from start to finish. I feel in this hour God is asking us to build on the foundation of Jesus Christ alone with the gospel of salvation and the kingdom as central to our mission. He wants us to finish well by ensuring He remains our primary focus. We are here to glorify God alone. It must be about Him not us!

In this hour, God is calling His children and kingdom leaders to relationally connect across denominations and prayerfully collaborate to transform their cities WITH Christ! You may be thinking, "How can one organization or individual transform an entire city?" Well, quite frankly no one person or organization can do it alone, but together a handful of kingdom leaders can! Prior to COGL's inception, when approaching potential participants, I heard leader after leader say things like, "It's impossible!" "I don't envy you; trying to get pastors and kingdom leaders to get along is a tough job." "There's no way you can get that many leaders to work together." Some even went so far as to say, "It's never going to work."

We can look back now and boldly proclaim, "With man this is impossible, but with God all things are possible!" (Matthew 19:26) We are celebrating more than a decade of service to the kingdom leaders in our region, and we haven't gotten here on our own! It's taken the investment of several years by key kingdom-minded leaders in our region; it has taken thousands of hours of face-to-face meetings; there were years invested in building trust, having conversations and praying together; and a multitude of time spent learning to listen in order to understand one another's callings, passions and gift sets. It took effort, humility, consistency, prayer, perseverance, and a willingness to work through perceived conflicts. It required each of us to bring our portion, share our hearts, speak the truth in love, and do menial tasks in service to the larger body of Christ! I am not going to say it was easy because it wasn't, but it's been well worth it. We are finally seeing a unity develop that transcends denomination, race, gender and generations. We are realizing we truly are one spiritual body in our city, and we are learning how to function in unity without compromising our personal convictions or blurring our primary passions. It's been a beautiful journey of discovering how the Church can function together in a city and how being connected to one another brightens our segment of the power grid and strengthens our corporate witness.

Perhaps you are on a journey or are being called to begin one. Who is God calling you to connect with? You don't have to journey alone; we've been created to travel together! So plug in to the unified Christian networks in your city and watch the Lord light you on fire for Him! Perhaps you don't have a unified network in your region. Ask God to lead you to individuals who share your kingdom passions. As we unite, we are built up into the fullness of Him who is the head, as iron sharpens iron. Everybody wins and God gets all the glory! "Because there is one loaf, we, who are many, are one body, for we all share the one loaf" (1Corinthians 10:17). After all, what do we have that we haven't received? (1 Corinthians 4:7) Since we have been given such a great and precious gift, namely Christ in us the hope of glory and the privilege of being called sons and daughters of God Most High, we must remember that it was indeed a gift — a gift we will give an account for one day. Being that we did not earn it and being that it is beyond measure in value, surely we will be accountable for how we shared it, multiplied it and freely gave it to others. I want to challenge you today to ask Father God how He wants you to connect with the unified expression of the body of Christ in your city. Ask God specifically how you can serve the corporate body in your region. If He doesn't answer you then you're off the hook. If He does, then just do whatever He shows you and say whatever He tells you to say. Father

God is inviting you to join Him in the greatest adventure of your life. Will you partner WITH Christ to transform your city?

## SYSTEMIC VS. PROGRAMMATIC

I am always intrigued to listen and learn how others sense God is calling them to move forward. I enjoy conversing with kingdom leaders, listening to sermons preached across diverse denominations, and, on occasion, looking for correlations in the questions that are plaguing kingdom leaders. I have had some concerns with the Church's prevailing fascination with big — big buildings, big numbers, big events, big return on our investments and big impact. Please hear my heart. I am not saying that events are wrong or big churches have missed God or that big buildings aren't given by the Lord. Neither am I saying that big impact isn't a great goal. What I am saying is that the body of Christ has become fascinated with BIG everything! The bigger, the better. What I see happening is that many are so distracted chasing the next best thing, the next trend, the next fad, the next big book, the next strategy, the next way of doing it that many are failing to simply do what God has already spoken to their hearts. I was once on staff with an organization that literally changed its vision statement three times in a five-year period. Every time a new leader would come in they would change the way they would walk out the vision. It was discouraging to those of us working in the organization because we would get the vision, get excited and begin to move forward and then in two years it would all change, leaders would be removed, programs would be canceled and we were back to square one. It was a bit like planting an oak tree only to uproot it every two years and move it to a different location. It makes it difficult for the tree to grow and take root. I once described it to a friend in that organization as being spiritually bi-polar.

There is great potential for impact in simply being clear on the "now thing" that God has called you to do. Sometimes our fascination with BIG actually derails us from our destiny, which is so often achievable through the simple obedience to the thing that is right in front of us! God says when we are faithful with a few things He will make us ruler over much! I have watched leaders come and go in our midst. The ones we are seeing experience the most success are simply doing the next thing God asked them to do over and over again. They day in and day out faithfully look at what they specifically and uniquely bring to the corporate body of Christ and they focus on it. I believe with all of my heart that each city has the very leaders within it who are called to transform that city WITH Christ! If you simply partner with one another, invite others with similar passions into your story, and are faithful with the little things then you will reach God's intended purposes for you. David sang it best in Psalm 138:8, "The Lord will fulfill His purpose for me; Your love, O Lord endures FOREVER; do not abandon the works of Your hands."

I believe that in our efforts to be organized, efficient and excellent the church has unintentionally made two grave mistakes. First, we have fallen into the deception that the body of Christ is an organization instead of a living organism. This belief has resulted in disunity, fractured relationships and immature converts instead of mature disciples of Christ. Second, we have inadvertently booted

56

Father God out of the driver's seat by attempting to lead, guide and direct our own destinies. So many of us are sincere, passionate and well intentioned, but in many cases we have taken the proverbial wheel and we are driving our own organizations, lives and ministries. I have to catch myself when I get in "just get 'er done" mode. I especially find that when I am weary, my tendency is to press in, persevere and produce. I am learning it is better to slow down, ask questions, check my heart and hear from the Lord the answer to the questions. The bottom line is that in western culture we have idolized progress, production, and profit over people. But Jesus didn't call us to build businesses. He called us to build up people WITH Him. It grieves my heart when I see organizations that use up people as a resource to accomplish the vision instead of realizing that the vision is a vehicle to serve the people. Quite frankly, it is downright dangerous. The mandate of Christ to leaders in the church is to equip the saints to do the work of the ministry. This work is more clearly defined in Ephesians 2:10, "For we are created in Christ Jesus to do good works, which God has prepared in advance for us to do." Notice these two things: God has a specific work for each one of us and He created us with that specific work in mind. In other words, even though an individual may not produce what we think they should, function how we think they could, or operate the way we do, it does not mean they aren't doing the very thing they were created to do. It may not look the way we think it is supposed to look or it may not grow as fast as we think it ought to, but that is not necessarily a bad thing. When we cease seeing people as being uniquely created for a very specific and vital work that progresses, changes, grows and morphs, we miss out on the creative genius of the divine destiny God created them with, the works prepared in advance for them. Christ has asked us as kingdom leaders to equip the saints to do the work that *He* has prepared for them prior to them being born. We are here to help them discover that purpose and fulfill that destiny in as much as they are willing to do the work. We are not here to call them to *our* vision, idea or grand plan. If you ask God to show you how to equip them, He will. Building our own kingdoms can be evidenced subtly in our mere impatience with others; as grotesquely as a lust for power; or even as deceptively as a desire for more, the new and the next.

From time to time, my husband Shane will share about dangerous situations at work and how procedures, safety and the care of the workers are the top priority. In a practical sense, all of us want to ensure we have electricity and water coming to our home; however, during an outage, customers get frustrated with the delay caused by taking the necessary precautions to protect the workers and avoid further outages across the city. There are so many parallels between Shane's job and the work I do. While funders often want immediate numbers, impact statistics, and event results, God has called us to do so much more than create catalytic events and programs that produce the statistical data required. He is calling us to create systems and change culture by strategically connecting kingdom leaders within the seven spheres of influence (Arts and Media, Economy, Education, Family and Neighborhoods, Government, Science and Technology, and Religion, as defined by Bill Bright and recently modified by Bill Johnson) across our entire city and help them learn together how to literally create kingdom culture within each sphere of influence. Culture change is a lofty goal; one that will result in cities and ultimately nations being transformed WITH Christ! There are many things that we can change if we are willing to follow the leading of the Holy Spirit! It is so important that we heed His voice and not simply chase this or that trend if we want to cooperate with God to do what He wants done. We don't have to worry about being first; we are yoked to the Alpha and Omega. He is literally the beginning and the end. He will have the last word. We do not need to know everything to do what God has asked us to do. We simply need to remain in close relationship with the One who knows all, who created all and who sees all — Almighty God!

# Chapter 7
## HINDSIGHT REALLY IS 20/20

We Americans love our high-speed internet and instant access that ensures the democratization of data nationwide. While I am not sure the majority of our citizens take full advantage of the benefits our freedom to information provides, it is always at our fingertips should we care to thoroughly investigate a matter ourselves. Quite frankly, an entire book could be written on the need for a societal shift away from making decisions based on the sound-bite segments we Americans are inundated with, but we'll save that for another time. This 24/7 access to information has created an interesting culture in that we have developed some norms that are not necessarily kingdom at the core. There is only one I would like to address here for our purposes, namely the unspoken expectation that one should be "in the know."

When we have conversations with individuals who say things like, "Haven't you heard that… (you fill in the blank)?" or "How could you not know that?" it is as if each person is supposed to be an expert in literally all things. There is a subtle message implying you don't measure up if you don't know and you should know because it is important information. These supposed nuggets of wisdom can be as trite as the scores in a ball game or as scandalous as unsubstantiated claims about a local celebrity or politician. I am not saying we shouldn't be in touch with reality nor am I suggesting we shouldn't keep abreast of newsworthy information. What I am saying is that no one person can be an expert on every subject, nor should we be. I believe our attempt to do so is actually pride masquerading as being well informed and fear and manipulation disguised as preparation and good practice. Dictionary.com defines an expert as a person who has special skills or knowledge in some particular field, making them a specialist or authority. The implication being that the individual is intimately acquainted with the field through BOTH knowledge AND experiential practice. The English word expert comes from the Latin word expertus, which literally means tried, proven and known by experience. In its purest form, being an expert requires an element of action, repetitive practice, and experience in a particular field. Webster's 1828 Dictionary is renowned as a unique and essential tool for educating Christians. It has the greatest number of Biblical definitions of any reference book and includes roots traced in 26 languages. It states that the word expert means properly, experienced; taught by use, practice or experience; hence, skillful; well instructed; having familiar knowledge of; as an expert, etc.

In the early years of COGL, we hosted catalytic events featuring leaders of large organizations and highlighting one major issue — for example, hunger — in our region. The intent of these events was to make a notable difference in the community, one that impacted the lives of both the recipients and the participants. We celebrate the fact that God graced us to feed more than 12,000 families and raise nearly $400,000 to stomp out hunger over the course of the three years we held the Food Drop. But looking back, these large events did not create sustainable transformation and culture change. While there were beautiful testimonies from both recipients and volunteers that their lives were deeply impacted, we were faced with the hard reality that these families were still hungry the other 364 days of the year. I knew we didn't have the expertise to create sustainable change, but I was determined to connect with those who did and discover what our next step was to bring true transformation.

Large-scale catalytic events like these are a great way to kick start a movement. They provide excitement, wow factor, and opportunities to connect with individuals who are truly passionate about the issue being championed. However, the death of a large-scale event focused around the same issue multiple years in a row is inevitable. They typically begin to taper off during the second or third year. We noticed the decline in our catalytic event we called the Food Drop in the third year and had to quickly decide if we were seriously committed to bring transformation or content with simply re-inventing another large-scale effort around a different issue. It became the season when callings were clarified. It was a necessary season that separated those who were interested in the platform, prestige and PR and who were merely infatuated with the idea of changing our city from those who were convinced our work was vital, who were committed to systems and systemic change and who were faith-filled and graced by God with the grit to move forward regardless of the risks. Much to my dismay, at that time we initially lost some of our largest funders. They were not interested in partnering with a longer-term vision. To their point, we did not at that time have an end date and had not yet clearly defined the vision because it was still morphing. Because we were intentional to maintain honoring relationships with these organizations, once clarity was gained these vital partners re-engaged with the work. We, of course, were ecstatic to welcome them back! Those who remained decided to dream big; trust God; and go after culture change, systemic change, and true transformation. It was a defining moment for many who were involved.

We were intentionally shifting from an organization known for one catalytic event to becoming a backbone organization that encouraged collaboration for the purpose of making a collective impact, cultural change, and an indelible difference. This was a major paradigm shift for many of our partners. We recognized the need for an organization to convene, connect and platform Christian leaders across the seven spheres of influence so we rebranded as the COGL Network and began cultivating leaders and serving the "important actors" as a backbone organization. We hoped the inclusion of the word "network" would further clarify our collaborative approach among local kingdom leaders that encouraged unity in the body city-wide and negated any sense of competition. Over time, it did help both current and potential partners to understand our new focus but it took several years for the community to understand our new direction.

You may be asking what is collective impact? Or what is a backbone organization? The winter 2011 issue of *Stanford Social Innovation Review* focused on collective impact, defining it as "The commitment of a group of important actors from different sectors to a common agenda for solving a specific social problem." Although it is a secular concept, collective impact can easily be applied to the Church. Each local church is important. Each one plays a specific and unique role within the regional community. In addition, the Church spans every sector of society and Christians hold many of the "important actor" roles in any given region. A backbone organization is simply one that is willing to serve the other important actors by hosting the events w62here they can collaborate, connect, create and convene. It is often led by various servant-hearted "important actors" in a specified region. What could be accomplished if each capitol city had a Christian organization that served the larger Christian body to collaborate, connect, create and convene? How would our nation be impacted if in each state Christians collaborated to impact their cities WITH Christ — advancing the kingdom of God together? You may be thinking is that even possible since we don't all agree. That is a valid point that I will address later, but let me assure you it is possible to unite without compromising your strongly held convictions.

There are five key conditions that distinguish collective impact from other types of collaboration: a common agenda, shared measurement systems, mutually reinforcing activities, continuous communication, and the presence of a backbone organization. In a follow-up 2012 article, *Channeling Change: Making Collective Impact Work, the Stanford Social Innovation Review* asserts that these five conditions "offer a more powerful and realistic paradigm for social progress than the prevailing model of isolated impact in which countless nonprofit, business and government organizations each work to address social problems independently. The complex nature of most social problems belies the idea that any single program or organization, however well managed and funded, can singlehandedly create lasting, large-scale change." And also with the Church, no single local church or ministry, however well managed and funded, can singlehandedly reach every person in a metropolitan area. We are compelled to work together! According to the *Review*, more and more people have come to believe that "collective impact is not just a fancy name for collaboration, but represents a fundamentally different, more disciplined, and higher performing approach to achieving large-scale social impact."

It was clear that Christians in our region already had a *common agenda* (defined by Scripture) and did many *mutually reinforcing activities*. It was also clear COGL had important actors from the public, private, and social sectors within each of the seven spheres of influence, which positioned us well to serve as a *backbone organization* in the region. But because of the lack of communication, much of the work historically was duplicative, disconnected and fragmented at best. The formation of COGL as a backbone organization solved the communication issue as we hosted a multitude of events to ensure *regular connection and communication*. Also, until 2013 we didn't have anything that would qualify as a *shared measurement system*. In April 2013, COGL launched a shared measurement system for Lansing through Meet the Need, a seamless solution for service and stewardship for the 21st century church.

According to Meet the Need Founder and President Jim Morgan, "Our mission is to get the church out of the four walls and into the community to show care and compassion to people who have needs. Then those people are more open to hear the gospel. Jesus rarely said who He was until He met a need. We have to do a better job of following that model." The goal of Meet the Need is to provide a shared measurement system that mobilizes more people to demonstrate God's love to others through acts of service.

After 10 years of development, Meet the Need was launched in 2013. Now working in cities across the country, including Lansing,

Meet the Need empowers charities, churches and businesses with the state-of-the-art platforms they need to manage and communicate all of their charitable activities. It automates the communication process and provides each church and charity with a single platform for managing volunteers, in-kind donations, families in need, events, drives, etc., saving money spent on purchasing and time spent learning all of those different systems. Practically speaking, Meet the Need integrates with any church website and connects the faith community directly to the preferred local nonprofits. For example, organizations can post their volunteer and resource needs and church members can search for ministry opportunities that fit their skills and interests.

What we love most about it is that there is no cost for the software or support. Morgan asserts, "Mobilizing and equipping the church to lead millions more to Christ by following Jesus' example of meeting those in need exactly where they are is what fuels us." We believe as cities shift to one regional service module this will decrease duplication of programs, increase nonprofit-organization visibility, decrease church administrative workload, encourage accountability with services provided, and empower passionate people to put their love in action. Ultimately, it frees church leaders to focus on equipping the saints to do the work, instead of organizing work projects for the saints so they can put their love into action. Your city can get more information about Meet the Need at meettheneed.org.

In two short years, COGL shifted from an informal movement known for doing catalytic events to being a non-profit network serving as the backbone organization for our capitol city and the surrounding region. We went from hosting big name speakers and well-known pastors and issuing press releases to recruiting and building strategic teams of local Christian practitioners who shared similar passions. When we made this transition to functioning as a backbone organization, the recruiting of leaders to form those teams within the seven spheres of influence was a bit tricky. I knew it would be presumptuous to create an agenda and call others to it assuming it would align with their passions, callings and kingdom mandates. In a moment of brief uncertainty, when leaders were hesitant to engage more fully, I had asked God how to make this work. I knew I was missing something. Then I felt He was leading me to consider more closely the gifts of those who were already serving in our midst. When I took some time to assess who was already helping with our various initiatives, I realized we had more than 55 volunteers who were deeply engaged. They were sold out to the vision of being United to Transform Cities WITH Christ. At the network events, we knew that connections were formed between leaders who wouldn't have otherwise met. We knew that interest was being piqued and small seemingly insignificant seeds of organic collaboration were beginning to germinate. But, that simple question — How do we make this work? — had started me on an extraordinary journey of discovering what God was doing in our midst and who He had already brought to help us build.

The next couple of years I had a multitude of one-on-one meetings and we continued hosting quarterly leadership summits, annual conferences and prayer gatherings, looking for the experts in our city. I was asking who has been doing focused kingdom work in our region for more than three years. If we were going to see real change take place, the agenda would need to be created by those important actors and be fully owned by them. Some of these important actors or experts had been working in their sphere for decades. Instead of orchestrating teams, we convened them around their area of passion. It was the only way to ensure everyone could stay focused on their individual callings and mandates and yet still give them ample motivation to stay at the table. We convened these experts together and after telling them to dream big, we asked them one simple question — What is God asking all of you to do together?

# Chapter 8
## LEADING LEADERS

When we first started gathering leaders, we had absolutely no idea what we were doing. We had stepped out in faith and were trusting God to make His continued direction for us obvious as we were faithful with each step. The mere diversity of the leaders we were considering presented some unique challenges. We knew they were the experts so rather than approach them with a plan, we decided to ask a lot of questions. We believed they were positioned to share how they had been successful in their area of expertise, and we believed if we worked together we would inevitably see the commanded blessing of Psalm 133:3b: "For there the Lord bestows His blessing, even life forevermore." Sounds simple, right?

While the concept certainly was simple, implementing it was not. It was comparable to getting my armpit waxed. I will clarify a bit for men reading this book. Imagine having a beautician place hot wax on a small portion of your beard. It burns a bit because it has to be warm enough to stick to the hair but you tough it out because you prefer not to shave every day. Then the technician proceeds to place a cloth on the hot wax and rub feverishly back and forth with a tremendous amount of pressure, practically bruising you in the process. But you think, "This will be worth it, I will be razor free for a month!" In a moment of panic you realize the hair is stuck to the wax that has just cooled and is now attached to the cloth strip! In pure survival mode, you have a moment where you just want to stop the process altogether, only to realize it's too late. The strip is already stuck to your face. You're relegated to the fact that it is too late to turn back. So you muster all your courage as you look into determined eyes and prepare for what you've convinced yourself won't be too bad! You start to think, "I can't believe that I paid someone to do this to me." Finally, the tech yanks the cloth with one quick move. The burn slowly sets in and your eyes tear up. You thank God that it's over. You relax and exhale a sigh of relief just in time to be reminded that the hair has to be removed from the rest of your face. Does that paint a better picture?

Convening strong leaders to gather for one purpose can at times feel a bit like this repetitive, painful process. We know the end result will have a lasting effect but the process of getting there will be messy and painful. A wise friend once said that vision is caught, not taught. With a vision to transform an entire city, it simply takes time for people to grasp it. Many sincerely want to help but need time to count the cost. It will eventually require an investment of their treasure. Ultimately, they have to weigh if it is the best use of their talents. I fondly refer to leaders who are "all in" as those who have passed the time, treasure and talent test. We term them as kingdom leaders and internally refer to them as those who are "in it to win it." These are leaders who understand that "team work makes the dream work — specifically God's dream for our city!" They value the corporate body of Christ in both thought and action so much that they regularly give of their time, treasure and talent to support His collaborative kingdom work in the region in addition to their personal ministry calling. I have found that this three-pronged litmus test, if you will, reveals the hearts of those truly committed leaders who have been awakened to and fully embraced their role in the regional body of Christ.

All joking aside, the most difficult and painstakingly long part of the process was scheduling the initial meetings and convincing leaders to attend. Quite honestly, for some of the teams it took me three and even six months to schedule the first gathering. These experts are passionate about their work and are often deeply engaged in the work on a daily basis so their schedules are tight. Overall, the search for the experts went well. We found that 55 of the leaders who were already working in our midst had passions spanning several of the seven spheres of influence. There were also several well-organized ministries who already had networks focused on specific initiatives. So rather than duplicate their work, we offered to partner with them. They welcomed the idea and we moved forward together. After several one-on-one meetings, these experts or regional practitioners agreed to convene. Many of the initial gatherings were spent listening and learning about those in the room. Because they were all passionate about the same thing, we simply asked them to share about their organization and how they were advancing the kingdom of God in their sphere of influence. It was a blast watching the room as their excitement increased at the potential to transform our city. In many cases we didn't have to ask them to take it to the next level, the leaders in the room almost always suggested a collaborative effort without any facilitation from us. We were simply there to introduce them to one another and to help each of them succeed. We rarely had to intervene unless a team got stuck. The same is true today. kingdom-hearted leaders are passionate about influencing our culture and the people in our cities for change, so often they simply need encouragement and connection with others who share their desire to dream big.

Early on it became clear that the movement could not be about a single personality. These leaders were already committed and had a wealth of experience in their designated fields. There would frequently be occasions when initiatives would warrant the advocacy of different leaders and their individual approaches. Each one of us was vital to the work. Each one had expertise, skills and connections that were vital to the mission to transform cities WITH Christ! We were intentional to recruit and partner with servant-hearted leaders. We had experienced a few instances early on where individuals were a bit too big for their britches, as my mom used to say. We found that the true experts displayed the fruit of the Spirit listed in Galatians 5:22-23, "Love, joy, peace, patience, kindness, goodness, faithfulness, gentleness and self-control" (ESV). These authentic servant leaders were humble, kind, gracious, encouraging, and so often in need of encouragement themselves. They were literally laying their lives down for the cause of Christ. Some had the typical titles, accolades, and fanfare, but so many of them were simply obedient to what God had asked them to do. Being an obedient servant had positioned them for the influence they now carried.

As the teams began to develop, I observed varied responses and inclinations in the hearts of those on each team. Some would assert that we needed to reach unbelievers, others would suggest that we needed to care for the Christians, while still others would say we needed to write down the process by which we were doing things. Outwardly, it appeared as though there was no unity in the room at all, which was at first a bit off-putting to those in the room; however, that was not the case. One of my favorite assessment tools right now is Alan Hirsch's *Forgotten Ways Assessment*. Coupled with *The Forgotten Ways book*, it provides some excellent assessment tools. What I like best about the assessment is that it seems to test for an individual's default function mode. We found his 5Q tools to be helpful in situations where we had passionate, pure-hearted Christians who had seemingly polarizing views on what should be the next steps. For us, it clarified that we actually didn't have disunity on the team at all, but simply people with multiple gifts sharing their varied perspectives. We could agree that each gift was needed to make the initiative a success. Once the distinction was made between different perspectives based on individual gifts verses perceived disunity on the teams, the progress accelerated. We were finally able to take some real steps forward.

Leading a city-wide movement has been completely exhilarating and if I am being honest, at times it has been absolutely exhausting. Over the last decade of gathering leaders, I have learned one thing for sure — we all have much to learn. There is something powerful in one's willingness to be determined to simply hang on and not let something go. The longer I work toward the goal of transforming cities WITH Christ the more I realize how much work there is to be done. I often thank God that we don't have to do it alone. In every city there are thousands upon thousands of passionate, pure-hearted, willing Christians just waiting for someone to help them discover who God created them to be. We as kingdom leaders are privileged to be able to journey with God's children to help them discover that they were created for a great purpose. It may not happen as fast as we would like it to sometimes, but it is always well worth any amount of pain, perseverance, and patient endurance. Hebrews 6:13-15 says, "When God made his promise to Abraham, since there was no one greater for Him to swear by, He swore by Himself, saying, 'I will surely bless you and give you many descendants.' And so, after waiting patiently Abraham received what was promised." So, keep doing what God has called you to do, keep being who God created you to be. Keep taking the next step of faith. One day, like Abraham, you too will receive what God has promised. God is good. He desires to give good gifts to His children. What next step is He asking you to take?

# Chapter 9
## THE EFFICACY OF VULNERABILITY AND TRUST

Since we had moved from an event-based organization to thinking more systemically, we needed to change the way we were connecting leaders in our network. Moving toward systemic culture change meant we would have to move beyond the traditional board-run approach of the typical non-profit. Initially, I just prayed, *Lord send help*, and He did. He sent precious individuals to serve on the board, as staff, and to come alongside me personally to respond to various needs of our quickly growing network. Internally, I began to ask God questions like: *What is it going to take to shift a culture? Where do we start? Who should I invite into this process first?* Prior to the solidification of our 501(c)(3), I felt compelled to gather five key leaders who specialized in coaching and organic church planting. These leaders were unique in the sense that they were already sacrificially serving regional organizations. They primarily felt compelled to help people reach their full potential in Christ through either discipleship or coaching. We were cut from the same cloth in that regard, but they had been at it a lot longer and I needed the wisdom God had imparted to them.

People come and go with movements like this one, but there are always those who become fully vested. One individual, Dennis Moore from Ministry Coaching Making Disciples (MCMD), was one who sat on that original team and proved to be a co-laborer when it came to building this movement. He served humbly, cared genuinely, pressed into me and other leaders appropriately, and engaged passionately in the work. He became so vested that he accepted a position on our board in 2017. I cannot think of one individual locally who has personally helped me and, in turn, the COGL Network more than Dennis. I will forever be thankful for his willingness to not only coach our leaders but also labor to see the vision come to pass. He coached me through various board, staff, friendship and re-organizational changes. He has proven to be an invaluable coach, friend and brother in Christ.

That said, if you are leading a movement or thinking about leading a movement, you will need a coach. There is a plethora of coaching organizations nationwide; coaching seems to be the new trend and many new organizations are being developed. They offer organizational and individual coaching. However, many I have encountered are focused on worldwide impact; organizational models; and increasing performance and production from your staff, volunteers and leaders. This approach mimics the American manufacturing mindset. It lends itself toward a cookie cutter approach that values replication, speedy production and performance over people. This approach often requires little involvement and investment of the leaders on the ground and simply isn't a kingdom approach. These values are completely contrary to a Christ-centered movement focused on personal and cultural transformation. What makes the situation with a local coach unique is that he or she is vested in the movement. Under the manufacturing model, oftentimes a coach will leave the ownership of the implementation in the hands of the leader. But having a local coach, who was accessible, invested and available to our team, was instrumental in our process and more closely models how Christ equipped His leaders as He journeyed WITH them on a daily basis.

Dennis has a powerful partner in ministry, Scott Rolff, who is the founder of MCMD, who has also labored hard with me in this movement — specifically with encouraging local pastors. One of the favorite things I have learned from these two leaders is the value of "going together" instead of alone. They have regularly challenged our board, team leaders and kingdom leaders in the community to go WITH others, referring to the example given by the life of Christ. Jesus had the three, the 12, the 70, and the 120 disciples. Together they ministered to the crowds, the cities, the lost and the hurting. Jesus rarely did any ministry alone with the exception of His personal prayer and fasting times with Father God. He had concentric circles of relationships with people who ministered WITH him. Through these faithful few, the entire world was impacted. We changed our tagline from the original "United to Transform Lansing for Christ!" to "United to Transform Cities WITH Christ!" because going WITH others and partnering WITH Christ became a core value and we wanted it reflected in our new tagline.

Shifting from a mindset of *me* to a routine of *we* requires intentionality, humility and often slowing down so the group can go together. Those who know me well would probably say I have a hard time slowing down. Practically speaking, I am not naturally slow but am instead frequently too fast in a team context. In Genesis chapter 33, Jacob says something to his brother Esau that jumped off the page at me one day. Jacob had originally fled his home and gone to his Uncle Laban's at the advice of his mother after he had deceived his father into giving him his brother's blessing; Esau had traded his rightful blessing for a bowl of stew. In chapter 33 of Genesis, Jacob is finally leaving Laban's house with his wives Rachael and Leah after 20 laborious years serving his father-in-law. Traveling with him are all their children along with the livestock he had acquired from Laban. To Jacob's credit, he did value the blessing more than Esau but he leveraged Esau's moment of weakness and hunger against him for his own personal gain. Needless to say, Jacob, now renamed Israel, was nervous about returning to be re-united with his brother, Esau. In these few verses, when they finally meet, Jacob is making several excuses as to why he does not want to go with his brother. But what he said in Genesis 33:13 was profound for me personally, "But Jacob said to him, 'My Lord knows that the children are tender and that I must care for the ewes and cows that are nursing their young. If they are driven hard just one day, all the animals will die. So let my Lord go on ahead of his servant, while I move slowly at the pace of the droves before me and that of the children, until I come to Seir.'"

Because of Jacob's track record with honesty, I actually researched this to make sure he was telling the truth. The American Journal of Obstetrics and Diseases of Women and Children, Volume 67, substantiates Jacob's story in both humans and animals saying, "The Shepherd protected the ewes from fright because it affected the lambs. The farmer boy was careful not to drive the cow home not to irritate her for fear of spoiling the milk. Yet how little care is taken for nursing mothers in this respect. He fully believed that a life devoid of nervous shocks was of far greater importance for the well-being of the nursing mother than a diet devoid of minor indiscretions." It goes on to say, "The metabolism they knew was often inhibited, the whole digestive process upset and the sweat glands inhibited or stimulated by emotion and yet they utterly ignored the emotional effect on the sensitive milk glands."

"I must care for the ewes and cows that are nursing their young. If they are driven hard just one day, all the animals will die...." When I first read these words in Genesis 33:13, I was convicted. Everything I did was fast and most of the time I would move faster if I could. It was like in that moment Father God was saying, *Sweetheart, I know you're in a hurry, but I am not. If you don't slow down my people are going to die.* Now I knew He didn't mean it literally, but He did mean eternal death. I stopped dead in my tracks. In a moment of spiritual sobriety, I began to see all the leaders as if they were pregnant with their destinies and callings and nursing those disciples in their primary spheres of influence. My heart broke. In a flash it became glaringly obvious — I had to slow down. My fast and furious approach would work when cleaning my house or meeting a deadline for my book, but it was not going to help these leaders give birth to and care for all plans and "good works God had prepared in advance for them to do" (Ephesians 2:10). If we were truly going to unite to transform cities WITH Christ, it would require not only going WITH others, but slowing down to their pace while encouraging, loving, feeding and coaching them.

The thing I love about coaching is that it is focused on the one being coached, not on the individual doing the coaching. The individual receiving the help actually sets the agenda, creates the potential solutions and takes ownership of the outcomes. This ensures you are not pushing the individual too hard, but simply partnering with the Holy Spirit to help them discover their next step toward Jesus. Coaching, quite frankly, is one of the most effective ways to transform lives and, in turn, transform city culture. In the fall of 2017, our Multiplying Transformational Relationships Team, fondly referred to as the MTR Team, joined the leadership coach training program facilitated by Mike Winter, an MTR team member and a director for Christian Business Men's Connection. Again, Mike is a local guy, with a great heart, doing great work and is invested in our city. Our goal moving forward is to create a coaching culture in the context of the network. This approach keeps Christ at the center and ensures we don't drive people but instead let God lead them.

The one thing every Christian leader can agree upon is that Jesus, the Son of God, was freely given for us and the world so that whoever would believe may receive eternal life (John 3:16). The Word of God says, "Now this is eternal life: that they know you, the only true God, and Jesus Christ, whom you have sent" (John 17:3). The words "that they know you" come from the translation of the Greek word ginōskō. It means to properly know, especially through personal experience, first-hand acquaintance, to experientially know. So, we see this idea again of knowing something personally, experientially, intimately. We look for leaders who know God in this way and who also are experts in serving in their sphere of influence. I believe it is impossible to truly know Christ intimately apart from being connected to His corporate body in your region. Even missionaries alone in remote areas are connected to larger Christian organizations to ensure they have some sort of support system. In our individual churches, often the majority of our members hold the same preferred doctrines, worship styles, preaching preferences and traditions that we do. Our love for God and others is tested in some measure in these controlled environments. Our love for God and for others can only truly be fully tested to a certain degree in the context of the regional gathering where others do not share our same intrinsic doctrines, worship styles, preaching preferences and traditions. We very quickly learn how intimately acquainted we are with Christ when surrounded by other Christians who hold beliefs and preferences contrary to our understanding of the Scriptures. When powerful leaders are added into the group, the differences can seem magnified at first. In these settings, do you find yourself encouraged, hopeful and willing to be in relationship with others? Or, do you feel uncomfortable, agitated and concerned about how their perspective is misrepresenting God? Or perhaps you prefer not to deal with it and avoid these situations all together. The question becomes how do we inspire leaders to be courageous and vulnerable enough to build high-trust relationships, especially with distinctive leaders with varied callings, gifts and passions?

# Chapter 10
## THE KEY — MAGNANIMOUS LIVING

I believe there is only one remedy that has the efficacy to establish the high-trust relationships among the diverse kingdom leaders in the midst of movements like ours, and it is magnanimous love! You may be thinking that sounds a bit naive, trite and over simplified. Or, surely she doesn't really think that love can change the world? But we as disciples of Christ must remember God says He is love. Love alone cultivates trust, which creates unity as relationships are forged. Picture the people of God taking the hand of God and then extending the same grace He has given us to each other and then to the world around us. We carry within us the very solution the world needs, namely Jesus Christ! Love is the essence of the Gospel. Each leader in a city carries a vital portion of Father God's kingdom vision for their city that no other individual can accomplish. There may be similar passions, but no two people are alike, no two callings are identical. They may be similar but will always differ in some way whether it is location, people group or even the impacting sphere of influence.

This love must be a sincere love, a generous love, a forgiving love, a gracious love and a patient love. There are many facets of magnanimous love. In this chapter, we will look at a few key aspects. Magnanimous love must be a love that seeks to hear the heart of another to understand their story, their journey and their divine dreams. In the relationally diverse contexts of unified movements of this magnitude, leaders are often on such opposite sides of issues that only their love for Christ can move them to commit to building His kingdom together. And only the love of God experienced through those in the group can convince them to be vulnerable and persevere.

Walking in magnanimous love cultivates a culture of freedom and divinely creative solutions that we could not otherwise reach if we remained separate. It doesn't mean that we run with every idea that is presented to our organization, but because of our love for one another we are supportive, encouraging and helpful to individuals who are passionate about things that differ from our passions. It requires a commitment to ongoing acts of excellent service.

My name has very special meaning to me. Stephanie means crowned one, Ann is grace and Butler translates to one who oversees those who provide excellent service to the master of the house. It literally means a crowned one of grace who oversees the excellent service to the master of the house. When the Holy Spirit first showed me this I laughed out loud. What if God isn't looking for more superstar ministries in this final hour, but instead He is looking for servants of excellence and humility committed to loving each other and the world in their city until Christ is exalted and God's kingdom is advanced?

I have been prayerfully reflecting on the cultural war being waged for our nation this year. My heart is stirred with a desire to see the body of Christ rise up to become the solutions the world is looking for today — solutions that exemplify the fullness of God's grace to us and display the lavish love of our perfect heavenly Father. We know that the same grace and power that raised Jesus from the dead dwells in us. We have great hope that it is not only possible, but reasonable to believe God desires to do the miraculous in our midst once again. Even while the entire world points fingers at our nation and reports we are no longer united but divided, God is at work in our cities. God is calling His people, and they are remaining intentionally united. He is calling us to stay the course. He is calling us to be deliberate in maintaining relationships with those who hold different political and denominational views or who look different. Many are asking, "Will the divine experiment of this nation that provides liberty and justice for all succeed?" We may very well be in the midst of our nation's greatest test; however, we are also at the precipice of an incredible opportunity! We know that the light always shines the brightest in the midst of a dark room. And in the same way, these very tensions are the necessary backdrop to highlight the grace, glory and goodness of God in this hour. Our nation desperately needs the body of Christ to live our love out loud!

## SACRIFICIAL LOVE

We need to walk in sacrificial love, meaning that what we do in this day and season ought to cost us something. The days of playing church and comfortably worshipping and advancing our own kingdoms have passed. It is time to ask God, *"What needs to go?"* and *"What's next?"* First Peter 2:20b-21 says, "But if you suffer for doing good and you endure it, this is commendable before God. To this you were called, because Christ suffered for you, leaving you an example that you should follow in His steps."

We were created to overcome. If we want to reach the nations with Christ, we can no longer make it about our comfort, our agendas, our ideas, and our way. Suffering for doing good is part of our call. Jesus suffered, and so will we. It will be well worth the cost to be able to stand before our Lord and hear Luke 19:17, "Well done, my good servant! Because you have been trustworthy in a very small matter, take charge of ten cities."

## GENEROUS LOVE

We need to walk in generous love, which means giving beyond the tithe. There are many organizations and groups that are advancing the kingdom of God. These groups are doing some of the work that the local congregation simply can't because the church is focused on getting people whole. These pioneers are out there every day taking the next mountain and partnering with God to transform the world. We must begin to consistently fund those movements that are changing cultures, changing lives, and changing systems. If we want to see cities transformed, then we need to dig deep and support those doing the work. However, this generous love must be lived out in our churches first. In Acts, the early Church went above and beyond to ensure that the believers in their community had everything they needed. In fact, they were so generous they even sold properties and possessions to ensure that needs were met. Acts 2:45 says, "They sold property and possessions to give to anyone who had need." Are there things you are holding onto that the Lord would have you sell to support someone in need? Are you looking for opportunities to give toward kingdom-hearted vision? COGL is always looking for new kingdom-hearted partners.

# COURAGEOUS LOVE

We need to walk in courageous love. The days in which we live are not for the faint of heart. Yet, when we look at the news stations and social media platforms, it seems that multitudes are dismayed by the battle being waged. This battle is the very thing we were created for! As a Christian you have exactly what you need to be victorious in the hour. The King of kings and Lord of lords lives inside each of us and has given us a mandate to go and make disciples of all nations. What an honor and a privilege! Some have bought into the deception that they do not fit the mold, look the part, or feel brave; therefore, they are not called to do great exploits for God. That simply isn't true! Look at every person of faith in the Bible; each one struggled, at some point, with courage. The Scripture says in Habakkuk 3:19 (AMPC), "The Lord God is my Strength, my personal bravery, and my invincible army; He makes my feet like hinds' feet and will make me to walk [not to stand still in terror, but to walk] and make [spiritual] progress upon my high places [of trouble, suffering or responsibility]!" In other words, God is our bravery when we feel faint, scared, paralyzed and inadequate. He is enough. You literally have everything you need to be brave in Jesus!

# MAGNANIMOUS LOVE

Finally, we need to walk in magnanimous love. This is the key! We must begin to love others the way Jesus loves them — sacrificially, generously, courageously, and magnanimously. We are the answer the world needs; we are the ones called to partner with the God who has a divine solution to every problem. He loves us all perfectly. What are we waiting for? Let's start a Love Revolution — one that first transforms the way we live personally, then transforms the way our local gatherings function, and then transforms the world one city at a time!

Through Christ, we have freely received redemption, forgiveness, hope, power, righteousness, peace, and joy and now freely we must give it. I am always amazed at how tightly we sometimes hold that same mercy that was freely given to us from others around us. As if, in the deep recesses of our mind, we believe we have earned it. Or even worse, perhaps we believe we are more deserving of it. But we aren't, are we? All have sinned and fallen short of the glory of God. There isn't a single person in the history of the world, apart from Jesus Christ, who never sinned. All sin separates mankind from God. Father God truly is no respecter of persons. His identical and perfect grace is available to terrorist and innocent child alike. We often hear about the last great end-time harvest. Many say it will be the largest harvest of souls in the history of the world. I believe that to be true. I believe we are already seeing this take place in other parts of the world: Africa, Iraq, Australia and South America. Many worldwide evangelistic organizations are seeing massive conversions and exponential church growth happen in these other countries. However, in North America, we are experiencing a decline in the Church and according to Barna Group only 55 percent of Christians are "churched," meaning they are connected to a local congregation. I believe we will only see a massive harvest as we Christians take a sobering look in the mirror and count the cost, resolutely deciding we will recklessly love this world. We will love them when we're persecuted. We will love them when we're humiliated. We will love them when our reputations are dragged through the mud. We will love them when they don't ask for it. We will love them when they mean us harm. We will love them when they steal. We will love them in the depths of their vileness and depravity. We must be willing to follow our Lord even unto death. We have gotten comfortable here in this land we call the land of the brave and the home of the free. We must remember how to fight the good fight of faith. We must be awakened again to the reality that there are truths and justice worth dying for. The time is now, not tomorrow, not next week, but today! In my spirit, I hear a resolute call to the troops saying, *Get up, get back to the front lines, time is short and our Lord is coming quickly!* Ask Him today, what's next? I humbly submit that the Church functioning corporately in a city is our single greatest witness (John 17:23).

## GOD GIVES GRACE TO SHIFT

*Lord, please show me any ways I have been lulled to a sleeping stupor by my daily comforts. Please baptize me afresh with a zeal for Your house. May I be consumed with Your heart for my city, my church, and the city dwellers there. Show me my portion. Help me to bring divine solutions to those in my sphere of influence, fill me with Your magnanimous love. Help me live sacrificially, generously and courageously so that many in my sphere of influence will come to a saving knowledge of Jesus Christ. Teach me how to partner with You to lead people into wholeness, into their divine destinies and back to You! And Lord have mercy on us, forgive us for being selfish, forgive us for being afraid, forgive us for being apathetic, forgive us for caring more about our ministries than Your kingdom. Change our hearts and glorify Your name fully! In Jesus' name, Amen.*

# A FEW SOBERING FACTS

- In the last 40 years, more than 1 billion people have died who have never heard of Jesus, and around 30 million people this year will perish without hearing the message of salvation. (Baxter 2007, 12)

- 70,000+ people die every day in the unreached world without Jesus. (Baxter 2007, 12)

- Christians make up 33% of the world's population, but receive 53% of the world's annual income and spend 98% of it on themselves. (Barrett and Johnson 2001, 656)

- North American and European Christians spend $12.5 trillion on themselves and their families each year. (Barrett and Johnson 2001, 656)

- Only 0.1% of all Christian giving is directed toward mission efforts in the 38 most unevangelized countries in the world. (Barrett and Johnson 2001, 656)

- Representatives of 60% of the world's nations live in the metropolitan area of Lansing, MI. (Wikipedia 2015)

- 22 million internationals visit the United States each year. Of these, some 630,000 are university students from 220 countries, 25% of which prohibit Christian missionaries. 80% of those students will return to their countries having never been invited to an American home. (The Traveling Team)

- 40% of the world's 220 Heads of State once studied in the United States. (The Traveling Team)

- 60% of international students come from the 10/40 Window. (The Traveling Team)

- More than 160,000 believers will be martyred this year. (The Traveling Team)

- Christians spend more on the annual audits of their churches and agencies ($810 million) than on all their workers in the non-Christian world. (World Evangelization Research Center

- Approximately 85% of all missionary finances are being used by Western missionaries who are working among the established churches on the field rather than being used for pioneer evangelism to the lost. (Yohannan, Revolution in World Missions, 143)

- One indigenous ministry surveyed the believers in the churches they planted and found that 80% had come to faith in Christ because they had seen a miraculous act of God or experienced an answer to prayer. (Chacko 2008, 138)

- That same indigenous ministry holds that their average missionary will plant three churches within the first five years on the field. (Chacko 2008, 138)

- The New Testament is translated into the languages of 94% of the world's population. (Johnstone and Mandryk 2005, 7)

- The potential audience for Christian radio programming is 99% of the world's population, assuming good reception, availability of a radio, and a desire to find the programs. (Johnstone and Mandryk 2005, 7)

- Two of the largest Gospel radio broadcasters, Far East Broadcasting Company and Gospel for Asia, both receive around 1,000,000 listener responses each year. (Far East Broadcasting Company, 15; Gospel for Asia)

- There have been 4.1 billion viewings of the Jesus Film, representing about 3 billion individuals. More than 99% of the world's population could view the film in a language they know. (Johnstone and Mandryk 2005, 7)

- In 2009 alone, Global Media Outreach, the internet outreach branch of Cru (formerly Campus Crusade for Christ), reported more than 10 million internet users came to faith in Christ through their websites. They also received close to 4 million emails. (Global Media Outreach)

- In one month alone, Trans World Radio saw more than 500,000 downloads in China of their online broadcasts. (Libby, 2)

# REFERENCES

- The Joshua Report, Barrett, David B., and Todd M. Johnson. 2001. World Christian Trends AD 30 - AD 2200: Interpreting the annual Christian Megacensus. Associate ed. Christopher R. Guidry and Peter F. Crossing. Pasadena, CA: William Carey Library, Wikipedia Lansing, MI.

- Baxter, Mark R. 2007. The Coming Revolution: Because Status Quo Missions Won't Finish the Job. Mustang, OK: Tate Publishing.

- Chacko, Jossy. 2008. Madness. Croydon, Australia: Empart.

- Far East Broadcasting Company. FEBC 2010-2011 Gift Catalog.

- Finley, Bob. 2005. Reformation in Foreign Missions. USA: Xulon Press.

- Global Media Outreach. About Us. http://www.globalmediaoutreach.com/about_us.html.

- Gospel for Asia. Reach Millions with your Radio Ministry. http://www.gfa.org/radio/radio-impact/.

- Johnstone, Patrick, and Jason Mandryk. 2005. Operation World. Tyrone, GA: Authentic Media.

- Joshua Project. http://www.joshuaproject.net/

- Libby, Lauren. 2010. President's Column. 2010 Annual Ministry Progress Report 31, no. 2, http://www.twr.org/resources/progress_report.html.

- The Traveling Team. State of the World. http://www.thetravelingteam.org/stateworld.

- Weber, Linda J., and Dotsey Welliver, ed. 2007. Mission Handbook 2007-2009: U.S. and Canadian Protestant Ministries Overseas. Wheaton, IL: Evangelism and Missions Information Service.

- Winter, Ralph D., and Bruce A. Koch. 2009. Finishing the Task: The Unreached Peoples Challenge. In Perspectives on the World Christian Movement: A Reader, ed. Ralph D. Winter and Steven C. Hawthorne, 531-46. Pasadena, CA: William Carey Library.

- Winter, Ralph D., Phil Bogosian, Larry Boggan, Frank Markow, and Wendell Hyde. The Amazing Countdown Facts. Pasadena, CA: US Center for World Mission. http://www.uscwm.org/uploads/pdf/adoptapeople/amazingcountdown.pdf.

- World Evangelization Research Center. An AD 2001 Reality Check. http://gem-werc.org/gd/findings.htm.

- Yohannan, K.P. 2004. Come Let's Reach the World. Carrollton, TX: GFA Books.

- Yohannan, K.P. 2004. Revolution in World Missions. Carrollton, TX: GFA Books.

# Chapter 11
## BEAUTIFUL GRACE

Some leaders struggle with organic movements because they don't have the plan laid out in front of them. They want to see the end from the beginning. They have bought into a business model approach and linked it to Christianity, the assumption being if I have a goal, regardless of whether it is a directive from God in this season or not, and I put my shoulder to the plow, I will see the desired outcome. This approach has subtle implications that there is some kind of formula that exists. The assumption is that clear goals, direction and clarity around where they are going are needed at the onset of any worthy endeavor in order for it to be successful! Please hear what I am not saying. I am not saying we shouldn't plan, I am not saying goals are bad and I am not saying clarity isn't important. What I am saying is that if we have it all figured out and can clearly see the end from the beginning, it is entirely possible that we don't really have a God vision at all! I am also saying that we can have a fantastic plan and well-crafted goals that are completely void of having asked God what He wants in any given situation.

God is infinite in His knowledge and wisdom and if we are going to partner with the creator of the universe in His awesome omnibenevolence, as He is described in the Scriptures, we had better get over the idea that we need to know it all before we start or we may never partner with Him at all. There is not one scriptural example where God painted a detailed picture of exactly where He was taking someone and exactly all they would have to endure to get there. Quite frankly, I think if He had shown me every little detail before we started this journey toward building a movement to transform cities WITH Christ, I likely would have tried to build it in my own strength instead of relying on Him every step of the way. We are called believers and quite frankly that means we must believe that we can indeed trust God in everything. There is simply no way around it.

I love the term omnibenevolent. It comes from the Latin *omni* meaning all and *benevolent* meaning good. Locally, we use a phrase, "It's all good" when someone apologizes for making a mistake and we want them to know we forgive them. In other words, God is working it all out, my trust is in Him. He's got me, so I totally forgive you, friend. He's my healer, my provider and my protector. No one takes my life from me, in fact I lay it down of my own accord. I know and trust God is always working it all out to my good, because He is literally goodness to the very core of His being. Dictionary.com notes that omnibenevolent is an adjective meaning all-loving or infinitely good used in reference to God. It is often used with regard to divine characteristics, whereby God is described to be simultaneously omniscient (all knowing), omnipotent (all powerful), omnipresent (everywhere present) and omnibenevolent (all loving). Even more importantly, the Scripture says, "The Lord is [unwaveringly] righteous in all His ways and gracious and kind in *all His works*" Psalm 145:17 (AMP; emphasis mine). Again, in 1 John 4:8 it is written, "The one who does not love has not become acquainted with God [does not and never did know Him], for God is love. [He is the originator of love, and it is an enduring attribute of His nature]" (AMP). Since we know

He is always good, all loving, all powerful, all knowing and everywhere present, we can always, always, always trust Him!

# GRACE TO LOVE EVEN UNTO DEATH

Finally, I believe we need to take a lesson from our Jewish friends in Israel. They are wise in that they actually raise their children to make great sacrifices for their country from the time they are very young. It is part of their culture. Because of the history of their nation, they understand something only a fraction of Americans still appreciate — specifically that freedom does not come free at all but at the high cost of many brave men and women. Every young man and woman is required to serve in their military. According to Wikipedia, the normal length of compulsory service is currently two years and eight months for men (with some roles requiring an additional four months of service) and two years for women. There is something to be said for the practice of conscription. It prepares these young men and women for the harsh realities that they and their countrymen must address daily. I would dare say that as American Christians we often faint in the hour of trial because of a lack of preparation and an inability to endure hardships. It isn't because we are cowards necessarily but I think many of our congregants have no grid of comparison for what true persecution, courage and sacrifice looks like. Israeli citizens are literally willing to die for what they believe in and we Christians could stand to have a bit more fortitude and willingness to live sacrificially. I admire the zeal with which the Jewish culture serves, worships and lives. A people so zealous for their beliefs that centuries after being exiled from their country they set their faces like flint to not only return to the land, but also to restore it to its former glory. Israel's Law of Return gives Jews and their descendants' automatic rights regarding residency and Israeli citizenship. Upon my visit to Israel, I was honored to meet a local Jewish man named Eran, He showed us pictures of the devastation upon their country's land and the deplorable desolation of it in 1882 when the first Jews "aliyah" or returned home. As we drove across the land, however, we saw green harvest fields, vineyards, avocado groves, fish farms and lush countrysides. The comparison was almost unbelievable. As an environmentalist, Eran was passionate about the land and the pure grit it took over the past 100 plus years to restore it to its original state. They had a long-term vision that required a generational approach to accomplish it.

What would it look like if we looked at our cities generationally? What if we were not simply satisfied with what we could or should accomplish in our lifetimes, but looked far beyond us and dared to dream about the distant future, assuming Christ tarries? What would the Lord ask us to do? How is He inviting us to partner with Him? We have the true gospel, a fire that cannot be quenched, the love of God in our hearts, access to the literal King of kings and Lord of lords. How can we sit on our laurels and allow evil to reign in our midst? I am not saying a military approach is the answer at all, but perhaps we could benefit from repositioning ourselves and our families from the comfort of suburbia where we have worshiped the last four decades and intentionally move into the cities that are falling apart because so few of us are willing to be God's preserving salt and light. Whether it is a city that's falling apart or one of the seven spheres of influence's moral decay wreaking havoc on the hearts and minds of our citizens, my heart cries out, where are the servants? What caves are we hiding in? Surely we see the problems, surely God is still speaking. What is He asking of you — of us? Loving Jesus doesn't mean we don't engage in the battle; we are called to fight the good fight of faith. It doesn't mean we sit by silently while all hell breaks loose around us. It most certainly doesn't mean we lie around and simply wait for our Lord to return while the world literally goes to hell in a hand basket! I believe we, as the corporate Church, will give an account for how we stewarded cities. Remember with me the teaching on the talents, Luke19:17 "'Well done, my good servant!' his master replied. 'Because you have been trustworthy in a very small matter, take charge of ten cities.'" The reward to the faithful steward was cities. God is passionate about cities, but we must pass the talents test first. What has he given you and have you done what He's asked you to do with it? We live in an hour where time is of the essence. We must speak the truth in love. We must learn to endure hardships. We must learn to love even the vilest of mankind. We must prayerfully ask God for the "now" strategies and build His kingdom and not our own. We must learn to gain the victory in the Spirit against our true enemy, the enemy seeking to destroy the souls of men, women and children and then extend mercy to those duped by his deceptions. If we fail to uphold righteousness and advance his kingdom in the land, we will be living in a very different world 40 years from now and the consequences will be grave, but quite frankly well deserved. If we do not take action in response to His directives we will have no one to blame but ourselves.

We must act, we must speak, we must stand, we must fight, we must do it all in love, and NOW IS THE TIME!

## GRACE TO GO BEYOND

If you prayed the prayer at the end of the last chapter, I challenge you to begin to journal the new ways God speaks to you. Especially record those things that speak to your passion. Buy a notebook to specifically capture these dreams, Scriptures, answered prayers and confirmations. If you prefer a more structured format, we do offer a companion journal that can be purchased called, *A Journey to Loving Magnanimously.* More information can be found toward the back of this book. Prayerfully consider the place you spend most of your time. Ask yourself how God would like to move right where you work or serve all week long. A wise friend once told me if Christians didn't just gather on Sunday and then scatter the rest of the week we could get a lot more done. What if we gathered in the workplace or neighborhoods where we spend 80 percent of our time during the week in addition to gathering with our local body of like-minded Christians on Sunday mornings? What could be accomplished if you knew who the believers were in your place of work, neighborhoods and organizations? What could be accomplished for God if you purposed to gather weekly, to pray for God's best, and to partner with God to create a culture of honor, humility, courage and kingdom righteousness? What would God do if even something as simple as Wednesday Bible studies were moved out of the church building into our workplaces and not for the purpose of building our local ministry, though that could be a bi-product, but for the purpose of transforming our cities? What if the purpose were to shift the citywide culture toward kingdom culture where righteousness, peace and joy reign? One where malicious, evil and vile behaviors are not merely tolerated but courageously and lovingly addressed? What if God began to speak to those assigned to work there, live there or serve there about ways He desires to move in their midst?

Did you know according to research by Barna Group that statistically 84 percent of Christians say they feel marginalized or sidelined in the marketplace? Also, 54 percent say they feel misunderstood, 52 percent share that they have endured persecution and 31 percent say they feel afraid to speak up in the workplace. In other words, kingdom leaders in the marketplace feel ignored, cast aside, persecuted, afraid, and misunderstood! I believe isolation is the enemy's tactic in the marketplace. If he can keep us separated, we faint. However, if we are intentional instead to rally under our one Lord, one faith, one baptism with one heart — we will see His kingdom culture come everywhere we go! Imagine what God can do in the midst of a united people. Barna Group reports that 45 percent of individuals who affiliate as Christians are not connected to a local church gathering. Barna calls them unchurched, but I prefer the term *undiscipled*, which means we, the church, need to re-think how we are doing life together. There is an entire segment of believers who are not connected and likely not being discipled well. It is impossible to grow in one's faith and remain strong in Christ apart from being connected to other Christians. One doesn't really mature apart from growing together!

# GRACE TO OVERCOME FEAR

The Scripture tells God's beloved "do not be afraid" more than 76 times. My favorite verse about this is 1 John 4:18 because it not only commands us not to be afraid but it also shares the antidote for overcoming fear. "There is no fear in love [dread does not exist]. But perfect (complete, full-grown) love drives out fear, because fear involves [the expectation of divine] punishment, so the one who is afraid [of God's judgment] is not perfected in love [has not grown into a sufficient understanding of God's love]" (AMP). Love is the answer! God's perfect, magnanimous, amazing love is for you and for me. When we have a full understanding of the magnitude of God's magnanimous love, fear has no lie in our minds upon which to build and therefore no power to pursue us to do anything but God's perfect will. The Lord terms you His beloved. In other words, you are "Be Loved" well by the One who loves perfectly, the One who never misses a beat and never makes a mistake. You may have a thousand reasons as to why you can't begin a group in your workplace or neighborhood running through your head. Perhaps the faces of those who would persecute you are running through your mind. Maybe doing so would require pruning something else out of your schedule. However, if we ever want to see real change, we will have to prioritize His kingdom above our own preferences and priorities. We may even need to cut a few things out of our schedule. These could even be seemingly good, fun, exciting things so that we can pursue the better, best and God thing. Good is the enemy of the best. At some point our faith has to mean something. It only takes one generation to change a nation! Consider for a moment others in your organization or neighborhood who likely feel the same way you do. Could you ask them to help you? Earlier we discussed the importance of journeying WITH others. In the context of the marketplace it is just as important. Earlier we discussed the context of a coaching relationship. Coaching is most definitely a vital part of journeying together. It helps to challenge us and motivates us to hear what God is speaking to our hearts at any given time. These midweek gatherings are intended to create a space in the workplace where Christians feel encouraged, supported and informed about issues that need prayer and transformation whether personal or corporate. There are a few fantastic tools out there. One is **WorkLife.org**, which has some fantastic resources for workers, groups and organizations to launch transformation groups. They offer morning devotions, study guides, Bible studies and more. If you are interested in starting a group, start by finding one other Christian in your workplace and asking them to do it WITH you, just once a week. I think you will be surprised at how many will say yes. Remember the statistics — you basically have a 50/50 chance when you ask someone to join you, so what do you have to lose? The worst they can say is no.

Another resource to assist in creating a group in the workplace is Ed Silvoso's book, *Anointed for Business*. It lays out an ideal study for discovering where a group is at and where they would like to go together. Silvoso cites that Christians in the workplace fall into one of four categories: 1. a Christian who is simply trying to survive, 2. a Christian who is living by Christian principles, 3. a Christian who is living by the power of the Holy Spirit, and 4. a Christian who is transforming their workplace for Christ. Once your group discovers which category everyone is in, together you can work through the process of becoming a group that is transforming your workplace for Christ! I find that Silvoso's book is helpful in large Christian organizations as well. Often in these larger organizations, the enemy has infiltrated during seasons of expansion or transition and has been allowed to wreak havoc unchecked. Leaders may not realize what has taken place until it is too late. We all know or have been part of organizations like these. They are the ones where you think, is this really a Christian organization? They often lack the character, culture and convictions of Christ. Some have even taken Christ out of their personal testimonies all together for fear of offending someone. Be encouraged, it only requires a remnant to shift these organizations back and re-focus them on God's original design for them. Our generation must begin to act or we could lose everything our nation's founders died to provide us: freedom, liberty and justice for all. I used to tell my daughter, you are braver than you think you are — Jesus lives in you. It is not too late, but we must each do our part now!

## GRACE TO CREATE A WOMB

Have you ever seen the "Life in the Womb" YouTube video (babycentre.co.uk/4-weeks-pregnant) that encompasses an entire nine months in a four-minute video? It's amazing the way God chose to design an infant in its mother's womb. When you watch it for the first time it initially looks like complete chaos. You see the fertilization of the egg, then watch as it attaches itself to the wall of the uterus. At first glance it looks more like a blob than a human, but it is in actuality a human. In God's infinite wisdom this apparent blob contains everything needed to create an absolutely unique human being. Although it's only the size of a poppy seed, a lot is happening. Cells are migrating to an area known as the primitive streak, and forming into three layers that will later become the baby's organs and tissues. In the top layer, a hollow structure called the neural tube begins to form. This is where the baby's brain, backbone, spinal cord and nerves will develop. Skin, hair and nails will also develop from this layer. The middle layer is where the skeleton and muscles grow, and where the heart and circulatory system will form. The third layer houses the beginnings of what will become the lungs, the intestines and the unitary system. You can find information on fetal development at www.babycentre.co.uk. These often over-looked details are essential to the current *life in the womb* debates. Some scientists would have us believe that because this fertilized egg doesn't look like a human that it isn't one at all. But that is not the case. The scientific facts actually support the opposing argument. If left alone, this precious formless multiplying mass of cells grows exponentially, beautifully and in perfect order until the culminating ninth month when a full-size infant sits in the sacred womb of its mother awaiting the moment of delivery. In fact, what some perceive to be chaos isn't chaos at all. It is beautiful grace. Grace beyond one individual's ability to comprehend. A growing grace, closely conducted by the all-powerful, all-knowing, all-present and all-loving God of all creation — YHWH Elohim.

Embracing these early seasons of uncertainty and small beginnings is crucial to positioning the corporate Church in the city to birth our promised Isaac instead of finagling only to find ourselves holding an Ishmael instead. We must embrace these unknowns instead of resisting them. We must step out in faith when our flesh cries, "You must be crazy." We must absolutely trust that God, our Father, the creator of the universe does know best and that He is always good. As we journey in absolute surrender we enjoy the privilege of participating in His glorious grace! We won't do it perfectly, but as long as we get back up, make it right and keep moving forward, God gets all the glory. When we unite as one body around the areas of our greatest passions, we establish spiritual wombs where God can create, dream and orchestrate His ingenious plans for our cities as each one of us brings the portion He has given us. We literally give birth to God-dreams, city-destinies and culturally divine movements that reflect His beautiful grace. It is not a matter of birthing for the sake of creating something new but listening, learning and leading WITH His heart, His desires in His timing, being fully convinced that His perfect love never ever fails. For far too long we have settled for business as usual, most often because it is clean, not as messy, and often brings with it a financial stability that is quite frankly comforting. If we are going to change the world, if we are going to be the generation that ushers in the King of kings we must do things differently. We must think outside the box. We must take God out of our proverbial boxes. We must take greater risks and we must do it together. In this hour, I believe God is inviting us to dream WITH Him. He desires to do above and beyond anything we could ever ask, think or imagine. Now is the time — not two years from now, not 10 years from now, but today. My final challenge to you is this question: Where is God asking you to join or create a spiritual womb for His beautiful grace to birth an Isaac in your city?

If you prefer a more structured format, we offer a companion journal that can be found at the back of this book called, *A Journey to Loving Magnanimously.*

# Chapter 12
## JOYFULLY GIVEN

I come from a long generation of those who have voluntarily served in the armed forces. Some favored the Navy, others the Marines, and still others the Army or the Air Force. Those who chose to enlist embraced the challenge to live in the constant tension between the very real hardships of war and the inexplicable joy that accompanied their fundamental belief that they were amidst a rare company of brave men and women called to the fight for the good of country and countrymen alike. They appreciated and understood that their service, while not always known or acknowledged by the masses, meant life or death for multitudes of oppressed peoples. They knew that they were not just wearing a uniform but instead protecting our country's freedoms and providing much-needed assistance to stabilize nations worldwide.

## JOY IN BEING LIKE-MINDED

Much like those who so courageously serve in the armed forces here in America, we too are soldiers in God's army in a very real sense. We are called to fight the good fight of faith, to lay down our lives daily and to even be willing to die for our beliefs. Sometimes I look at the landscape of our *Facebook church, Twitter rants, big means it's better*, and *it's all about me* ministry pervading our nations and I think, *Lord, forgive us. Where are the Pauls, the Peters, the Junias and the Jeremiahs? Where are those who are completely sold out for Jesus? Where are the Daniels, who would take the lion's den over compromise? Where are the Moses? Those who would rather "be mistreated along with the people of God rather than to enjoy the fleeting pleasures of sin"? The daughters and sons who regard "disgrace for the sake of Christ as of greater value than the treasures of Egypt," because they are looking ahead to His reward? [Hebrews 11:25-26] Where are the masses of believers who through faith conquer kingdoms, administer justice, and gain what is promised; who shut the mouths of lions, quench the fury of the flames, and escape the edge of the sword; whose weakness is turned to strength; and who are powerful in battle and rout foreign armies? [Hebrews 11:33-34]*

I have found no greater joy than running with a company of people who are pure, passionate, purpose-driven, Christ-focused, and uncompromisingly willing to unite for the glory of God. I believe each city has them. In your personal sphere of influence, there are burning ones. I have the honor to know, love and work among many of them in our capitol city of Lansing, Michigan, and across the state. I humbly and lovingly submit, it is high time we Christians start working together — especially those who haven't joined the fight! If we are ever going to reach the utter most ends of the earth, we must focus on Christ, whom we have in common, and begin working together. We must be willing to fight WITH our brothers and sisters on the frontlines of the cultural wars being waged on our freedoms. Our freedoms to worship freely, to protect life, to define marriage, to ensure true justice, to care for the least of these, to uphold righteousness, and to equip believers for the reality of the culture wars they face daily. The whole nostalgic approach to our Christian thinking has got to change. We are long past the day of *this is the way we go to church, just put on our Sunday's best, sing a few songs, tithe, pray, us four and no more* mentality to Christianity. We can no longer live that way and in good conscience say we've fulfilled our Christian duty or our kingdom mandates. In these last days, it is simply not going to cut it.

The prophet Haggi says it best, "This is what the Lord Almighty says: These people say, 'The time has not yet come to rebuild the Lord's house.' Then the word of the Lord came through the prophet Haggai: *Is it a time for you yourselves to be living in your paneled houses, while this house remains a ruin?"*

Haggi continues, "Now this is what the Lord Almighty says: "Give careful thought to your ways. *You have planted much, but harvested little.* You eat, but never have enough. You drink, but never have your fill. You put on clothes, but are not warm. You earn wages, only to put them in a purse with holes in it."

This is what the Lord Almighty says: "Give careful thought to your ways. *Go up into the mountains* and bring down timber and *build My house,* so that I may take pleasure in it and be honored," says the Lord. "You expected much, but see, it turned out to be little. What you brought home, I blew away. Why?" declares the Lord Almighty. "Because of my house, which remains a ruin, while each of you is busy with your own house. Therefore, *because of you* the heavens have withheld their dew and the earth its crops. I called for a drought on the fields and the mountains, on the grain, the new wine, the olive oil and everything else the ground produces, on people and livestock, and on all the labor of your hands." [Haggi 1:1-11]

We are being called to be ambassadors, SENT INTO the mountains of influence to be ministers of reconciliation. *The Kingdom of*

*God* IS Righteousness, Peace, and Joy in Holy Spirit. He's sending us out to compel them to come in and, *not only be saved* from their sin, *but also be fully restored* and *sent back out* to reach others. A common misnomer about unity movements is that we must all be doing the same thing to be "one." It simply isn't true. This verse shows us that while we are literally one body, we do not all have the same functions. Working with other church, ministry, and marketplace leaders has brought me more joy than anything else I have had the privilege to do. There is nothing more exciting than listening to leaders passionate about their particular call to share the good news, create hope, and reconcile others to Christ in creative ways. The diversity isn't frustrating at all when we maintain Father God's perspective. His perspective highlights the vitality of His children's callings. He chose each person before the foundations of the earth to be born in their time. He gave them the desires of their heart and made them in His image to glorify His name. He issued them a divine invitation to present others with an opportunity for eternal redemption, absolute wholeness, and, best of all, to be in relationship with Him. Unity movements are absolutely inspiring. They exemplify most beautifully God's extravagant love for all humanity and His masterful orchestration of time, destinies and eternal invitations.

## YOU BELONG

We briefly covered this idea earlier in this book. I love the NIV version here because it captures the heart behind the original language when it says, "In Christ we, though many, *form one body*, and each member *belongs* to all the others." Romans 12:5 Whether it is convenient or not, the scriptural reality is that we are ONE BODY, and when one member, limb, or body part is hurting in the natural, the rest of the body *literally belongs* to the others. Therefore, in an emergency, it does whatever is necessary to ensure the entire body is healed, protected and properly diagnosed. The nerves alert the brain, the red blood cells and white blood cells seek to stop the immediate damage, the hands stabilize the limb, and, well, you get the picture. In the natural, the fact is the other members rush to the aide of the broken leg to ensure it is protected until it can heal. If we can prioritize others in these moments, it demonstrates in both our word and deed that we *belong to all the others* in the corporate body of Christ. Only then we can begin to see each other as vital parts of Jesus, and only then will it free us to begin to love each other well. Jesus laid down His life for ours. He has asked us to do the same for each other. It is a sobering thought, when we embrace this reality that we actually do *belong to one another*, but one that brings our Father deep joy. "***By this*** everyone ***will know*** that you are my disciples, ***if you love one another***" (John 13:35).

## COUNT THE COST

I had traveled to Ireland for the first time in May 2018. I knew God wanted me to pray at the top of Croagh Patrick, but I had absolutely no idea what getting there was going to entail. I was prepared only by a few prayers, two specific dreams, and a pair of confirming words through friends. Ten years after I had received the first dream, a door of opportunity opened, and I knew it was time to go. Ireland is a beautiful land, with a rich history of a precious people, historically wearied by the frequent onslaughts of enemies desiring to "overtake" their land, as the Irish like to say.

The truth is, I underestimated the fitness, skill, and effort it would require to climb Croagh Patrick. For some reason, when God asked me to do it, I simply thought, *Well if He asked and I am willing then by His grace I should be able to do it.* The hard reality of what I had agreed to do began to set in only 40 short minutes after embarking on the two-and-a-half hour climb up the five-mile trail toward the 2,405-foot peak. I had already climbed what seemed like hundreds of stairs, jumped around a plethora of large boulders, and gingerly made my way around trickling waters all while trying to keep my footing on loose rock. At this point, my two friends who were going to attempt to climb it with me were completely exhausted from all the maneuvering and a bit intimidated by the increasing incline that looked like a landslide of loose rock. They decided instead to wait below at the visitors building and pray fervently for my safe return.

When I originally said, "Yes, Lord, send me," I assumed it would be a leisurely climb up a scenic "bit of a hill," as the locals like to say. I thought it would allow for precious, prayerful reflection upon the purpose of the journey, but it was a far cry from a leisurely climb. More accurately, it was a treacherous trek up a rocky landscape at a constant, steep incline into increasingly high altitudes that made it difficult to breath. After managing to climb past the bottom one-third of the mountain's terrain, I hit a steeper incline that consisted of a wide trail covered in loose rocks. That portion of the climb almost did me in. I was taking 10-15 steps forward and then resting for at least 60 seconds before being able to continue onward. Every step I took had to be settled before I could put my weight on it, so as not to go sliding backwards and losing ground I had fought to gain. It was during this portion of the climb that my legs began to shake from weariness of the now one-and-a–half-hour journey. If I was going to complete the climb, I needed to pause for a 10-minute break to simply recuperate, re-hydrate and refocus on the task still at hand.

## LABORING TO REST

The summer after I returned from Ireland, at the recommendation of a close friend, I had a meeting with Kevin Defrees. He is a world-renowned mountain climber who led the charge for the team who discovered Noah's Ark. He has climbed five of the seven continental summits, skied to the North Pole, and searched for Noah's Ark as a lead mountaineer featured in the award -winning documentary *Finding Noah*. As I shared my story with him, he said "Stephanie, there is a technique we teach in mountain climbing called the rest step. You should research it. It is essential so climbers can rest the major muscles as they climb more difficult mountains."

He suggested I Google it and learn a bit more about it, so I did. It led me to Active.com. They have a wonderful article on the rest step that was written by Jeff Doran. He reports that, "Proper hiking technique is crucial to safety, preventing you from injury." He continues by sharing that, "The 'rest step' is a technique used by hikers to slow their cadence, rest their muscles and conserve their energy while trekking on steep terrain at high altitudes. Essentially, the rest step takes pressure and strain off your muscles and transfers it to your bone structure."

Just like we need to take a rest step in the practical sense when embarking on a mountain climb in the natural, we also need to take proverbial rest steps when advancing the kingdom of God in the seven spheres of influence. There were times when we were building teams, having conversations, asking people's opinions, and laying the foundation for this new expression of the corporate body in our city when I would feel wearied by the absolute vastness of God's vision for our city. Or even times when I would feel completely isolated because so few could grasp the big picture as their primary passion was to one particular area or another. I could see so clearly at times the ingenious intricacies and divine appointments that God was masterfully executing. And yet, there were seasons when it simply wasn't time to begin connecting certain groups together. Just like the physical body can only take so much strain on its muscles when climbing mountains, the body of Christ also can only apply so much truth at a time. If we move too fast or push too hard too soon, the leaders will become weary, worn out and overwhelmed. As a network we literally needed to rest, celebrate and enjoy what God was doing in our midst before pressing on again. These moments of resting in the reality that He was pleased by our partnership to love and care for His body brought us such encouragement of heart and much needed strength to continue the forward journey.

There are almost always mixed responses to the work God is doing in our midst. There are those who are shouting for joy, excited about the unity and feel it is an absolute answer to prayer. However, there are also very well-meaning leaders who have led movements in the past who look at this new movement and struggle with the organic feel of it all. They genuinely miss the impact numbers, the large events, the programs, the public reconciliation meetings and the platform approach to prayer. What God is building in our day doesn't look like the movements of the past because he is doing something new. This struggle isn't unique to us. Those in Ezra's time had to pass this same generational test. In Ezra 3:10-12, the foundation of the new temple had just been completed, and the responses of the leaders were not consistent across the collective group. It says, "When the builders laid the foundation of the temple of the Lord, the priests in their vestments and with trumpets, and the Levites (the sons of Asaph) with cymbals, took their places to praise the Lord, as prescribed by David king of Israel. With praise and thanksgiving they sang to the Lord: 'He is good; his love toward Israel endures forever.' And all the people gave a great shout of praise to the Lord, because the foundation of the house of the Lord was laid. *But many of the older priests and Levites and family heads, who had seen the former temple,* **wept aloud** when they saw the foundation of this temple being laid, *while many others* **shouted for joy."**

## THE JOY OF THE LORD IS OUR STRENGTH

Almost inevitably, those who have toiled and plowed and prayed to see past movements succeed will struggle with their first glance at the seemingly insignificant foundation of the next movement. And in Christ, there is always a next movement. And by next movement, I do not mean an extra biblical movement, nor do I mean one beyond Christ Himself and His finished work. He is the movement. However, as culture changes and Christ in His infinite wisdom uses a new wineskin, He still calls us to go and make disciples and that never changes. As the corporate body applies the wisdom received from the previous generation, the glorious germination process of the next new thing God wants to do begins. At the same time, so much work has gone into what God was doing previously. So often the cost of the blood, sweat, tears and prayers sown to see the last movement bear fruit can make the transition painful for those leaders who paid the steep price. I can imagine it would be difficult for the leaders of the past expression of a gospel movement to embrace what's next without mourning at least a bit over what was before. Foundations don't look like much. They look small in stature, they're tedious to build, and not flashy at all. The work needed to put them in place requires us to get down in the dirt, work with our hands, and look a bit undignified at times. Digging deep is a necessity, laboring to find the perfectly cut stones and embracing the patience required while each one is formed, fashioned and fitted for its position is vital. And while well-laid foundations do not tower and draw the eyes of mankind, they go deep and are built of the very bedrock of Christ, becoming the platform on which magnificent structures shall rest. Our spirits get excited about the idea of building foundations, but the realities of getting down in the mud, muck and mire can sober one's fascination with it pretty quickly.

When we have been so touched by the inexplicable, perfect, tender, bold, magnificent love of God, bringing him joy becomes our greatest achievement. There are so many ways we can bring Him joy.

Whenever we partner with Him to allow His magnanimous love to flow through us, we bring Him joy. The scripture says the love of God HAS BEEN poured out in our hearts through Christ Jesus our Lord (Romans 5:5).

The NLT version puts it beautifully in Romans 5:2: "Because of our faith, Christ has brought us into this place of *undeserved privilege* where we now stand, and we *confidently and joyfully* look forward to sharing God's glory."

It is when we recognize that we did nothing to earn the privileges by which we now stand in Christ that we are inspired to confidently *and* joyfully look forward to sharing God's glory with others. Overwhelmed at the goodness of God toward us, our own thankfulness cannot be contained and overflows almost uncontrollably into the lives of those around us. The NLT version goes on to say in verses 3-5, "We can rejoice, too, when we run into problems and trials, for we know that *they help us develop* endurance. And endurance develops strength of character, and character strengthens our confident hope of salvation. And this hope *will not lead to disappointment.* For *we know* how dearly *God loves us,* because *He has given us* the Holy Spirit to fill our hearts *with his love.*"

He has given us the Holy Spirit to fill (or for the purpose of filling) our hearts with *His love.* We joyfully look forward to sharing His *glory* in every circumstance. This is the confidence we have in Christ Jesus when we face various trials of many kinds. The joy of the Lord and the love of God in our hearts has sufficiently equipped us for every trial. Therefore, we can "Always be joyful. Never stop praying. Be thankful in all circumstances, for this is God's will for we who belong to Christ Jesus" (1 Thessalonians 5:16-18). First Corinthians 13:4-7 breaks love down into very specific actions. We often mystify love as if it is some abstract emotion or feeling, but clearly it has very specific actions associated with it, which you and I can enjoy! At times we the church act as though perfect love in and of itself is unattainable, but is it really? Beloved, I humbly submit to you that when you regularly encounter the perfect love of God in and through Christ Jesus you can experience inexplicable joy in loving those around you in an ever-increasing measure.

## JOY IN PATIENCE (V4)

Our adversary, the devil, prowls around like a roaring lion seeking someone to devour with his lies (1 Peter 5:8). Very often he will attack in a way that tempts us to be impatient with others. But love is patient and willing to love others while they journey through the process of discovering the same goodness and grace of God we have so freely received. Let's pause here and take just a moment to think back upon your own life. Ask God to show you the times when He has been patient with you. What did you remember? Do you think you can extend that same patience to someone you may be struggling with today? In light of His grace toward us we can be joy filled while being patient with others.

## JOY IN KINDNESS (V4)

We can also be tempted to be unkind to others for various reasons. Perhaps they have been rude to us and we want to lash back at them. But love is not easily angered. And that love fills our hearts. Maybe someone is experiencing success in an area we want to be successful in and we are feeling a bit jealous. But love does not envy. A healthy-hearted brother or sister is genuinely excited for their sibling when they are succeeding. The expanse of God's riches and wealth are quite frankly unfathomable. Our Father God can literally create worlds with His words. He has immeasurably good plans toward us as His children. He quite literally has an endless supply of good things to lavish upon each of us, so we do not have to be petty nor competitive over who gets what. We need only ask our Father for those things we desire. He longs to give good gifts to you. You are His child, and He loves you perfectly.

# JOY IN KEEPING NO RECORDS (V5)

This one took me a while to learn. I am Irish after all. In my family, records of wrongs was a specialty and it often determined the future of our relationship going forward. If you had earned our trust, it was of greater worth than gold in our eyes. Now, I am not saying we should maintain relationships with others blindly tossing boundaries out the window. There is wisdom in having appropriately strong boundaries with individuals who are physically dangerous or regularly untrustworthy and hurtful by breaking their word. We will discuss that later in this chapter. However, we can take joy in offering grace anew every morning.

One encounter with Jesus can completely revolutionize a person's heart. In hope, we can joyfully expect that something has changed and, without doubt, know that the blood of Jesus has covered the sins of their past. If you find yourself needing help with an especially traumatic experience, like I did in a difficult season, hold fast to this encouragement in Colossians 3:13. The Good News version tells us to, "Be tolerant with one another and forgive one another whenever any of you has a complaint against someone else. You must forgive one another just as the Lord has forgiven you."

A glimpse at God's grace toward us can quickly sober our thinking toward another person who has wronged us. Ephesians 2:4-5 GNB, "God's mercy is so abundant, and His love for us is so great, that while we were spiritually dead in our disobedience, He brought us to life with Christ. It is by God's grace that you have been saved." I, like Peter in Matthew 18:21-22 would argue with God, *Once I can forgive, twice maybe, but, seriously, Lord, more than that I just don't know.* If God graced me to walk in magnanimous love, He can change you as well. Be encouraged. You can overcome anything you are willing to face WITH Jesus.

## JOY IN THINKING ON THE PRAISEWORTHY

If you stay in ministry very long at all, there will come seasons when you praise the Lord in spite of those things you can see, hear, taste, touch, smell and discern. A faith beyond your senses begins to be awakened. No one told me this when I first said yes to the Lord. But persecution comes because of the word. We can take it as a compliment that our very real enemy sees us as a threat. This sobering truth is nestled in the midst of a completely different message in Mark

4:7, "But since they have no root, they last only a short time. When **trouble or persecution comes because of the word,** they quickly fall away." As soon as we get the word and we give our yes, the battle begins, and the ability to find something praiseworthy in a person during such an affront is one of the greatest weapons we have against the enemy of our souls. Discovering a person's unique purpose and praising God for the potential within them can completely turn the tide of a seemingly insurmountable onslaught. They of course are free to choose to respond to His beckoning voice, but God always works all things together for good. The commander of the army of the Lord told Joshua that he is neither for us nor for our enemies. See Joshua 5:14-15. God's concern is reconciling men to Himself and building His kingdom! Finding those things that are praiseworthy refocuses our thinking heavenward and keeps us focused on building His kingdom instead of our own.

Praise gives us those dove's eyes mentioned in Song of Solomon 1:15 that are stayed on our love and gazing upon His beauty. It keeps us focused in the heat of a battle, much like a soldier who has a picture of his loved one while away at war, to remind him why He's fighting. That picture gives Him the courage required to march into the onslaughts ahead. Our steady gaze upon the Lord as we praise Him focuses us on our source of all strength, peace, grace, goodness, and the originator of our directives. God asked us to be ambassadors, *these ones are the very reason we are here.* As we praise Him in the midst of the battle, we remember why we agreed to fight in the first place. The love of God overpowers the impending fear, and we march onward into whatever may come knowing Jesus conquered all our enemies at the cross, and He did it for those opposing us as well. He not only *was* our savior but He *is* our savior right now! And He longs to be their savior as well.

## JOY IN PRAYER & FAITH

Back in Ireland, while I was climbing Croagh Patrick, my friends Natalie and Ron were waiting for me at the bottom of the *bit of a hill* when I returned from the five- hour hike. When I finally met up with them and was able to retire my walking stick, you would have thought they had climbed the mountain with me. They were ecstatic. They celebrated with me, hugged me, encouraged me and laughed with me. I was absolutely exhausted, but they were full of joy. They had an inexplicable joy because they had partnered with me in prayer. They couldn't wait to hear the stories about my little adventure. They were looking on from a distance, and thought they saw me fall a couple times, but they were not sure if it was me. They displayed such a deep level of concern, compassion, and friendship, I was genuinely touched. I felt so loved, so honored, so cared for in that moment.

I learned that a local man had given them a pair of binoculars so they could search the landscape and potentially catch a glimpse of my progress. At the bottom of the mountain, this gentleman was explaining how dangerous this trek could be, and yet they simply stayed in faith and continued to pray. Writing this paragraph now, I am realizing my favorite friends are those who are full of joy. When I look at their lives, they have learned to persevere in prayer and life until they experience breakthrough. They have seen their prayers answered over and over again. They have an admirable quality about them. A generosity that goes beyond the ability to explain and a courage that bids me to believe for the impossible.

Much like the local man did for my friends, God has given you a pair of binoculars to be able to see things from His perspective. There may be someone whispering stories about how unlikely or dangerous or impossible it would be for God to intervene, but you just keep looking through those kingdom binoculars. Keep hoping, keep believing His word, His promises and watch Him grace those around you to climb mountains and reach unfathomable heights for His glory's sake. Stay in FAITH and remember with God all things are possible.

# CHAPTER 13
## JOYFULLY STANDING

It seems to be in vogue to be disagreeable these days. Mainstream media outlets appear to relish in running stories where disagreement, debate and distasteful displays of contention and accusation abound. There is nothing more exhausting than working with people who are simply disagreeable for the sake of being disagreeable itself. The scripture calls it a contentious spirit. It sounds trite, but seriously, aren't we all adults here? Can't we all just get along? I am joking, of course. The fall of man has created multi-faceted systemic fractures that have devastated people groups and entire community cultures. They took time to deteriorate and it will take time to redeem those who have been entrenched in them for generations. The Webster's Revised Unabridged Dictionary gives three definitions for contentious:

> *1. Fond of contention; given to angry debate; provoking dispute or contention; quarrelsome.*

> *2. Relating to contention or strife; involved in or characterized by contention.*

> *3. Contested; litigated; litigious; having power to decide controversy.*

In other words, a contentious person or organization is one who is fond of contention, given to angry debates, and known for provoking disputes. They are quarrelsome in a way that creates strife displayed by their regular involvement in issues of debate or litigation on matters where they exhibit behaviors suggesting they have power to decide on a matter of controversy. Are a few organizations or individuals coming to mind?

The Word calls this a *contentious spirit*. There is a spirit operating behind individuals and organizations who display these characteristics. There are 11 occurrences of the word contentious in Scripture. In Philippians 2:14 of the Weymouth New Testament (WEY) version, sometimes referred to as the Modern Speech New Testament of 1903, we are admonished to be "ever on your guard against a grudging and *contentious spirit*." In 1 Timothy 3:3 ASV, we are instructed that elders ought to be *"gentle **not** contentious."* In 1 Corinthians 11:16, Paul instructs those in Corinth facing a regional debate about women being required to cover their heads saying, "But if any man *seems contentious*, we have no such custom, neither do the assemblies of God." We are commanded to guard against this spirit because it can cause division across the body of Christ infecting an entire city, region, state or nation.

Finally, in the book of Titus, Paul is giving instruction to Titus, his "true child of a common faith" (Titus 1:4), urging him to exhort those in his midst to be godly and encourage "sound doctrine" (Titus 2:1). God's purpose is to raise up a people who have been purified "unto himself a people for his own possession, zealous of good works"(Titus 2:14). Paul's closing remarks give an accurate analysis of how we should deal with this spirit. I believe a critical spirit coupled with a spirit of contention is permeating the world's culture today and attempting to influence well-meaning Christians. To grasp the gravity of the situation and conversation it is important to look at Titus 3:2 in the context of 3:1-11. Paul starts with an admonition to bring firm correction to a specific group of people, *"Put them in mind to be in subjection to rulers, to authorities, to be obedient, to be ready unto every good work, to **speak evil of no man**, not to be contentious, to be gentle, showing all meekness **toward all men**."* Here Paul clearly defines that he is referring to a group of people who were speaking evil of others and being contentious. It is clear there was a group who was causing a problem in the body. Then he immediately encourages Titus to extend the grace of God to them as well. Titus 3:3 continues that thought, "For we *also once were foolish*, disobedient, deceived, serving diverse lusts and pleasures, living in malice and envy, hateful, hating one another. But when the kindness of God our Savior and His love toward man appeared, not by works done in righteousness, which we did ourselves, but *according to his mercy he saved us* through the [a]washing of regeneration [b]and renewing of the Holy Spirit, which he poured out upon us richly, through Jesus Christ our Savior; that, being justified by his grace, we might be made [c]heirs according to the hope of eternal life. Faithful is the saying, and concerning these things I desire that thou affirm confidently to the end that they who have believed God may be careful to [d]maintain good works." (Berean Literal Bible Version)

Remember, Paul was once so deceived that he literally hunted Christians down and murdered them. Therefore, the fact that he reminded Titus that he was once foolish was intentional. In fact, in

Acts 22:20 he said, "When the blood of your martyr Stephen was shed, I stood there giving my approval and guarding the clothes of those who were killing him." All this happened while he claimed to be serving God. So more than anyone else, Paul understood that a person could be zealous for God and sincere in their beliefs and, yet, completely deceived to participate in horrendous acts against the body of Christ. The intention of his heart here was to instruct Titus to respond firmly but with grace.

In Philippians 2:2 Paul exhorts the church to *"Make my joy complete* by being *like-minded*, having *the same love*, being one in spirit and of one mind." There is a fine line between individuals who are speaking the truth in love and those who are simply partnering with a spirit of contention. We can be joyful in being like-minded because we ourselves have been comforted by His love and encouraged by being united with Christ, and, in turn, joyfully have the same love, being like-minded, therefore becoming more and more of one Spirit (namely His) and of one mind (that of our Lord and Savior Jesus Christ).

## JOY IN BOUNDARIES

All this talk about love may cause one to think that love is all grace and no grit, but that certainly is not the case. Paul closes his letter to Titus with this sobering command "These things are good and profitable unto men: but *shun foolish questionings, and genealogies, and strifes, and fightings about the law; for* **they are unprofitable and vain.** *A factious man after a first and second admonition [e]refuse; knowing that* **such a one is perverted**, *and sinneth, being* **self-condemned**." In other words, when it comes to contentious people, you only give them two chances before separating from them — at least for a season. Of course, we ought to always lead with love because God is love (1 John 4:8). It isn't just a quality of God but God is literally love, so as His representatives we should be loving. Furthermore, we know that love is the only thing that never fails (1 Corinthians 13:8). Therefore, we freely extend the grace we ourselves have received in hopes that individuals will respond favorably to it (1 Corinthians 2:12). However, when we have extended grace, when we have been kind, when we have conversed and all this has not resulted in unity, reconciliation and like-mindedness, then separation is healthy. There comes a time when it is more loving to limit an individual's influence and access to us and our relational networks for the best of all involved. Boundaries with others are healthy, helpful and biblical. My favorite book on boundaries is written by Dr. Henry Cloud and Dr. John Townsend, co-authors of several books including a New York best seller called *Boundaries*. Dr. Townsend wrote a wonderful article that gives the simple scoop on the biblical basis for boundaries. Here is a portion of it (the full article can be found at https://www.cloudtownsend.com/scoop-on-boundaries/):

> "Simply stated, it is this: people have a need to be in control of their own lives, and they have a need to know that God is behind that idea. This need is fundamental in the creation of mankind, according to the Bible. God created us to be free, and to act responsibly with our freedom. He wanted us to be in control of ourselves, and to have a good existence. He was behind that idea all along. But as we all know, we misused our

freedom and as a result, lost it. And the big fruit of this loss of freedom was the loss of self-control. We have felt the results of that ever since in a wide variety of misery. Consider a few of the alternatives to self-control:

- Controlling relationships where people try to control each other

- Faith that is practiced out of guilt and drudgery instead of freedom and love

- The replacement of love as a motivator with guilt, anger and fear instead

- The inability to stop evil in significant relationships and cultures

- The inability to gain control of our own behavior and solve problems in our lives

- The loss of control to addictive processes

- The generational cycle of sin unable to be broken

These are to name a few. So, it is now no wonder why the need for Boundaries was felt so deeply. It is something so dear to the heart of God that He says it was one of the motivators for the sacrifice of Christ Himself: *It is for freedom that Christ has set us free.* **Stand firm**, *then,* *and* **do not let yourselves** *be burdened again by a yoke of slavery.* (Gal. 5:1). Jesus died to set us free: from sin, from the devil, from the world around us. And that is the essence of what Boundaries teach— freedom."

If we are going to reach the world with the gospel we must learn to limit evil in our midst — both in our own personal lives and in our spheres of influence where we have responsibility and authority. Having boundaries doesn't mean we don't give second chances but it does mean there may be seasons where we cannot or should not work with certain groups for the sake of preserving like-mindedness, unity and peace in our midst.

# JOY IN STANDING

If we aim to do great exploits in the name of our God we must learn to do the next, the new, the not-yet-done kingdom things. We must be able to stand before our God in good conscience able to say, not my will but your will be done. We need to be able to take an honest look at our lives and answer the question: Is what I am building for His kingdom or mine? God is eternally creative, good, compassionate and loving. He has plans for us that are beyond anything we could ever think of or imagine. What would it look like to begin to partner with Holy Spirit to accomplish noble dreams? If all things are possible with God, and they are, then what are we waiting for? What's stopping us? If you could do anything and you knew you wouldn't fail, what would you attempt to do for God's glory? Would you ask God to help you do just that?

I think often times we stop dreaming because it can be painful to do so in today's world. Many in America have been softened by our *fast-food, fast-paced, instant gratification, iPhone, Instagram* society. The moment something isn't picture perfect or starts running a bit slow, or, worse yet, breaks, we are programmed to toss it out and get a new one or just upgrade to the newest model. But people aren't programs, phones or editable photos so we cannot just filter out their imperfections. Some things cannot be rushed and cultivating trust and building Christ-like character are two of those things.

Learning to love magnanimously takes time; commitment; and a lot of often initially unwelcome, difficult, seemingly impossible situations in order to master it. Remember the story of Stephen? He was a man full of God's grace and power who performed great wonders and signs among the people (Acts 6:8). However, opposition arose from among the members of the Synagogue of the Freedman (Acts 6:9). Then they persuaded some men to say that they had heard Stephen speak blasphemous words against Moses and God, stirring the people and elders up until they brought Stephen before the leaders (Acts 6:11-12). Scripture states that they said his face was like that of an angel as they looked upon him (Acts 6:15). There's something about the love of God that changes our countenance. It makes the supernatural quality of who God is tangible. It allows God's glory to radiate and fill a room. It can change an entire atmosphere. Sometimes we are put in impossible situations and no matter how loving, how gracious, how forgiving we are, some may still sneer, gnash their teeth and be intent to stone us (Acts 7:1). Remember in those moments that hurting people hurt people. In those moments, often we only have fractions of a second to decide if Jesus is worth dying for. Ultimately, He died for us and there may come a time when we have an opportunity to die for Him. The question is, will you? Whether the opportunity presents itself to figuratively die or literally lay your life down, the question remains, will you? When you settle that question, there isn't much that can shake your faith. Once we decide that, whatever He asks us to do we will do it regardless of the cost to us, our ministry, our reputation, our relationships. The moments or rather opportunities to love magnanimously are reduced to a simple and unwavering, yes.

While he was being stoned, Stephen was full of Holy Spirit and had an open vision as he looked up into heaven. He saw the *glory of God* and Jesus *standing* at the right hand of God (Acts 7:55). If there is one thing I could leave with you, one short-cut if you will, to obtaining the grace to persevere into all the fullness of those things God created you to do in Christ Jesus, it is this — Love magnanimously. Find your strength in the joy of the Lord as you simply stand no matter what comes against you. And know that in those moments when you have done everything to stand, stand firm still. It is enough (Ephesians 6:13b-14a). This is how we change cities, norms, cultures and reconcile men to God. We stand when we are misunderstood, we stand when we are criticized, we stand when we are hurt, we stand when we are lied about, we stand when we're persecuted, we stand in God's magnanimous love for others. Persecution provides the perfect platform for us to give glory to His name. When we simply stand and trust Him with the outcome, we get glimpses of His glory and Jesus Himself stands and calls all of heaven's attention to look upon the one who looks like Him. Remember our heavenly Father is a rewarder and He is good. Remain standing, Soldier. Your reward will be great.

Beloved this is the "good fight of faith" and the very purpose for which we stand, "so that Christ may dwell in *our* hearts through *our* faith. And may we, having been [deeply] rooted and [securely] grounded in love, *become* fully capable of comprehending with all the saints (God's people) the width and length and height and depth of His love [fully experiencing that amazing endless love]; and [that *we* may come] to know [practically, through personal experience] the love of Christ which far surpasses [mere] knowledge [without experience] that we may be filled up [throughout *our* being] to all the fullness of God [so that *we* may have the richest experience of God's presence in *our* lives, completely flooded with God Himself]." (1 Timothy 6:12, Ephesians 3:17-19 AMP *Italics edited to personalize quote.*) This is our high calling, this is the aim of our faith - to be filled up to all the fullness of God, who IS LOVE and who has loved us so magnanimously. He is asking us to be Sons and Daughters displaying His Magnanimous Love for all the world to see!

# A Journey to Loving Magnanimously
## Companion Study Guide

## CHAPTER 1

1. Take a moment and ask God the following question. Father God, what is the one word you want to say to me right now?

2. Now look up the definition of it and write it below.

3. Based on that definition, do a word study using Scripture. Great tools are biblegateway.com or biblehub.com. Type in the word and see what God has to say about it. As you look and listen, ask yourself the following questions:

    a.   Who are the characters in the Bible God spoke this word to?

    b.  What are their stories?

c. How can you relate to their stories?

d. What does this story tell me about God?

e. What does it tell me about myself?

f. What's my part and what's God's part?

# CHAPTER 2

1. What aspect of the definition of magnanimous love did the Holy Spirit use to touch your heart?

2. In what ways has God asked you to give generously to others? Or is He prompting you to give generously to others now and if so how?

3. Who are those in your current spheres of influence that the Holy Spirit is asking you to love magnanimously?

4. Ask the Holy Spirit for specific ways to love them. When could you do what God is asking you?

# CHAPTER 3

1. Can you think of a time in your life when God pushed you out of the nest and you resisted? Or are you experiencing that now? If so, explain.

2. What did you or are you struggling with the most about this uncomfortable transition?

3. Ask God right now how He wants you to respond in this situation.

4. What does Joseph learn at the end of his journey about who allowed all the trials in His life? (Genesis 37, 40, 41 and Psalm 105:19)

5. What did Joseph learn about himself? Genesis 41:16

# CHAPTER 4

1. When it was all said and done, what did Joseph learn about God's plan? Genesis 50:19-21

2. How did this revelation give Joseph the grace to love his brothers? Who is God asking you to love today?

3. In what ways is God asking you to move forward? Read Exodus chapter 14.

4.  In what ways has God given you everything you need to do what He's asking of you? Read 2 Peter 1.

# CHAPTER 5

1.  Where (What sphere) (where do you spend 80% or more of your time) has God called you to go to war (in a spiritual sense) and defeat the evil pervading your immediate culture?

2.  What is the one battle you know you were created to fight for the sake of Christ's name?

3.  Who is God using to protect you or get you to your destiny that the enemy has tried to get you to hold offense against? Will you love them? Will you forgive them? Will you trust God?

# CHAPTER 6 and 7

1. How are you connected to the corporate body of Christ in your city?

2. Are you connected to those outside of your denomination?

3. In what ways does the story of the American dream contradict God's kingdom call on the life of an individual?

4. Who is God asking you to partner with so that you are not going alone but instead going WITH others? Who are those who share your same passion? When could you ask them to prayerfully consider going WITH you?

5. What is the difference between systemic and programmatic approaches? What are the benefits of each?

6.  What are some systems you have an opportunity to influence? Ask God ways you can use programs to catalyze teams passionate about systems, kingdom and culture change?

# CHAPTER 8

1.  Where has God positioned you to lead leaders, either current leaders or future leaders?

2.  In what ways can you help those leaders be passionate about who God has called them to be and still honor others with varied callings in their midst?

3.  What is a promise God has made to you? And what does his word say about it in Hebrews 6:12?

# CHAPTER 9

1.  Why is trust between leaders working together so important?

2.  What happens when the leaders do not trust each other?

3.  How can we as leaders of leaders intentionally create cultures where high trust is a value?

4.  When working with leaders of varied capacity, what truth did Jacob share about the flocks that is important to keep in mind? What happens when we do not follow his example?

# CHAPTER 10

1.  Where is God asking you to embrace some unknowns in your midst that may at this time feel chaotic? Can you trust Him to move in them?

2.  What are the four key facets of magnanimous love? And why is each one vital to a transformative movement seeking to change cultures?

3. What are the other important aspects of magnanimous love mentioned that were not expounded on? Why are these also vital to a transformative movement?

# CHAPTER 11

1. Meditate on the truth that God is omnibenevolent meaning He is all-loving or infinitely good. How does that challenge your perspective on an issue you have been struggling with?

2. Since God is always good and always working things out for good ask Him to show you how He is good in a specific situation you have been struggling with and write the answer below.

3. Stop and take a moment to consider how your response to this struggle could affect the generations beyond you? Think through the possible responses? What would be the outcomes?

4. Now ask Holy Spirit who He is His best possible outcome? Are you willing to do what's best according to Philippians 1:9-11?

5. Are you willing to lay your life down for your faith?

6. Why or why not?

7. What does that mean?

8. What would it require for you to say yes?

9. Ask Holy Spirit to increase your faith to do great exploits in God's name?

10. What are some ways you have gone beyond your comfort zone to advance the kingdom of God in the seven spheres of influence wherever you spend 80% of your time?

11. Ask God what He wants you to do next and how you can reach more people and have a greater impact? Will you do it?

12. When you think about stepping out what fears get stirred up in you?

13. What's the lie you are believing?

14. What's the truth?

15. What could it look like if you were to partner with others to create a spiritual womb in your sphere of influence? Dream a little. What would you pray, do, study, encourage, address, advocate for?

# CHAPTER 12

1. What are some areas where you are have opportunities to experience the joy of the Lord right now? (being like-minded, faith, prayer, showing kindness etc.) List one area where God is stretching you and write a prayer asking Holy Spirit to fill you with more grace and love. Ask God to help you see the situation from His perspective.

2. What are 10 things you are thankful for and 5 things you can praise God about?

# CHAPTER 13

1. If you were going to ask God to help you have the faith to stand in one area what would it be?

2. Ask Him to show you how to stand in this situation? Listen what is He telling you?

3. Now ask Him to send others or show you others who would be willing to stand with you. Write down their names He shows you. Can you contact them to set up a meeting and share your heart and vision within the next 14 days?

4. Ask God what you should share with them when you meet: Write your points below:

5. Pray for these meetings and ask God to prepare your heart and theirs.

*Stephanie and a team of regional leaders do offer coaching to leaders in Capital cities worldwide.

For more information contact us at **shekhinahchurch@gmail.com**
Subject: Coaching to Transform Cities WITH Christ!

35689590R00087

Made in the USA
Columbia, SC
22 November 2018